For Paul—
A glorious book for
a glorious man.
With much affection,
Michael

THE HASTINGS HOURS

THE
HASTINGS
HOURS

A 15TH-CENTURY FLEMISH BOOK OF HOURS

MADE FOR WILLIAM, LORD HASTINGS

NOW IN THE BRITISH LIBRARY, LONDON

78 PAGES REPRODUCED IN COLOR

PREFACE AND COMMENTARY

BY D.H. TURNER

THAMES AND HUDSON

*Reproduced from Additional MS. 54782 in the
Department of Manuscripts, the Reference Division,
the British Library*

First published in the USA in 1983 by Thames and
Hudson Inc.,
500 Fifth Avenue, New York, New York 10110

Library of Congress Catalog Card Number 82–74548

Typesetting in Great Britain by Keyspools Ltd,
Golborne, Lancs
Colour origination in Switzerland by Cliché Lux S A,
la Chaux-de-Fonds
Printed in Switzerland by Imprimerie Paul Attinger SA,
Neuchâtel
Bound in The Netherlands by Van Rijmenam b v,
The Hague

CONTENTS

Acknowledgments

Grateful thanks are returned to the British Library Board for permission to reproduce the manuscript. For particular help and encouragement gratitude is also expressed to Miss Janet M. Backhouse, Miss Shelley M. Jones, and Mrs Ann Payne, of the Department of Manuscripts, the British Library; to Mr C.A.J. Armstrong, of Hertford College, Oxford; to Dr G. Dogaer, Conservateur des Manuscrits, the Bibliothèque Royale Albert Ier, Brussels; to Dr M.L. Evans, of the Walker Art Gallery, Liverpool; to Dr Eva Irblich, of the Handschriften- und Inkunabelsammlung, Österreichische Nationalbibliothek, Vienna; to Dr T.J. Kren, of the J. Paul Getty Museum, Malibu; and to Professor O. Pächt, of Vienna.

Preface

✥

WHEN Duke Charles 'the Bold' of Burgundy married Margaret of York, the sister of King Edward IV of England, in 1468, the splendour of the festivities, which continued for nine days, taxed even the powers of the heralds to describe; and Englishmen declared that the magnificence of the Burgundian court was paralleled only by that of King Arthur. The Flemish painter Hugo van der Goes was employed on the decorations for the wedding; one of those present was a Welsh knight, Sir John Donne, for whom Hans Memlinc painted the Donne Triptych, now in the National Gallery, London. Sir John was the brother-in-law of William, Lord Hastings, the chamberlain and friend of Edward IV, for whom apparently, was made in Flanders – in Burgundian territory, that is – the beautiful manuscript book of devotions which is reproduced in the present publication.

Fine hand-made books, ornamented with miniatures and decorative initials and borders, were about to disappear as a major form of art, but before they did so, they enjoyed a glorious coda in the work of the Flemish makers of books in Bruges and Ghent. It is on the pages of their products that the middle ages seem most accessible to us, and the illuminated manuscript in general has become for us the characteristic artifact of the whole mediaeval period. Although the majority of illuminated manuscript books were religious in content, the pictures in them portray the secular as well as the sacred. The inclusion of genre scenes, and comical, satirical, even rude subjects, in illumination appears to have originated in England in the mid thirteenth century; over the next hundred and fifty years it developed into the vignettes of contemporary life which are such a feature of Flemish illumination. In the margins of the Hastings Hours a lover and his lass boat back from maying, largesse is thrown to the people, two knights joust, and the royal barge of England plies the river.

The Ghent-Bruges school is the culmination of Flemish book-painting. The Hastings Hours is datable before 1483 – as William,

Lord Hastings, was beheaded at the instigation of Richard, Duke of Gloucester, the future King Richard III, on Friday 13 February of that year – and is therefore the first of the school's surviving masterpieces. We know the names of some of the leading Ghent-Bruges miniaturists, such as Gerard Horenbout and Simon Bening; but the artist of the Hastings Hours is anonymous. There are, however, reasons of style and iconography for identifying him as Simon's father Alexander, the brother- (or nephew) in-law of Hugo van der Goes.

The Hastings Hours has been little studied or reproduced, but knowledge of it is vital for appreciation of the Ghent-Bruges school of Flemish manuscript illumination, and beyond that of early Netherlandish painting in general. As a historical document the Hastings Hours is fascinating because of its association with the England of the Wars of the Roses, of Edward IV, Richard III and the princes in the Tower. Edward and Richard were Renaissance figures; Henry VI, whom they deposed, had been a mediaeval one. Lord Hastings himself was perhaps more a man of the middle ages than of the Renaissance, and it is a world in transition that looks out at us from the pages of the Hastings Hours, a world that was striving to reconcile tradition and invention, decorative art and art for art's sake.

ix	f	viiii	
	g	vviii	
xviii	A	vvi	
vi	b	vv	
	c	viiii	
viii	d	vm	Vigilia.
iii	e	vii	Thome apli
	f	vi	
vi	g	v	
	A	iiii	Vigilia.
viv	b	vm	Nattuitas dñi.
viii	c	vii	Stephani prothom'
	d	vi	Johanne euuang'
xvi	e	v	Scorum innocax'
v	f	iiii	Thome cantuariess
	g	iii	
viii	A	ii	Siluestar pape.

12b

Initium sancti euuangelii secundum Iohem. Gloria tibi dne

In principio erat verbum. Et verbum erat apud deum z deus erat verbum. hoc erat in principio apud deum omnia per ipsum facta sunt et sine ipso factum est nichil. Quod factum est in ipso vita erat et vita erat lux hominum et lux in tenebris lucet et tenebre eam non comprehenderunt. fuit homo missus a deo cui nomen erat Iohannes. hic venit in testi

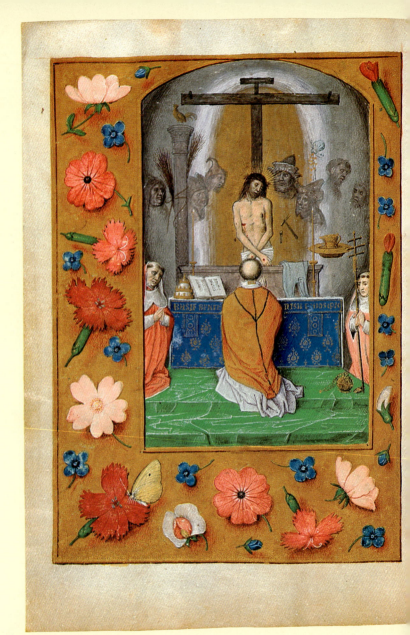

18b

Memoria de sancta trinitate.

Domine deus
omnipotens
pater et fili
us et spus
sanctus. da
michi fa-
mulo tuo. N. victoriam contra
omnes inimicos meos vt non
possint michi resistere neqz
nocere nec contradicere. sed
deijciatur virtus eorum et
consilium in bonum. Tu deus sis fortitudo mea et refu-
gium meum et eripias defen-
sionis mee et virtus immo

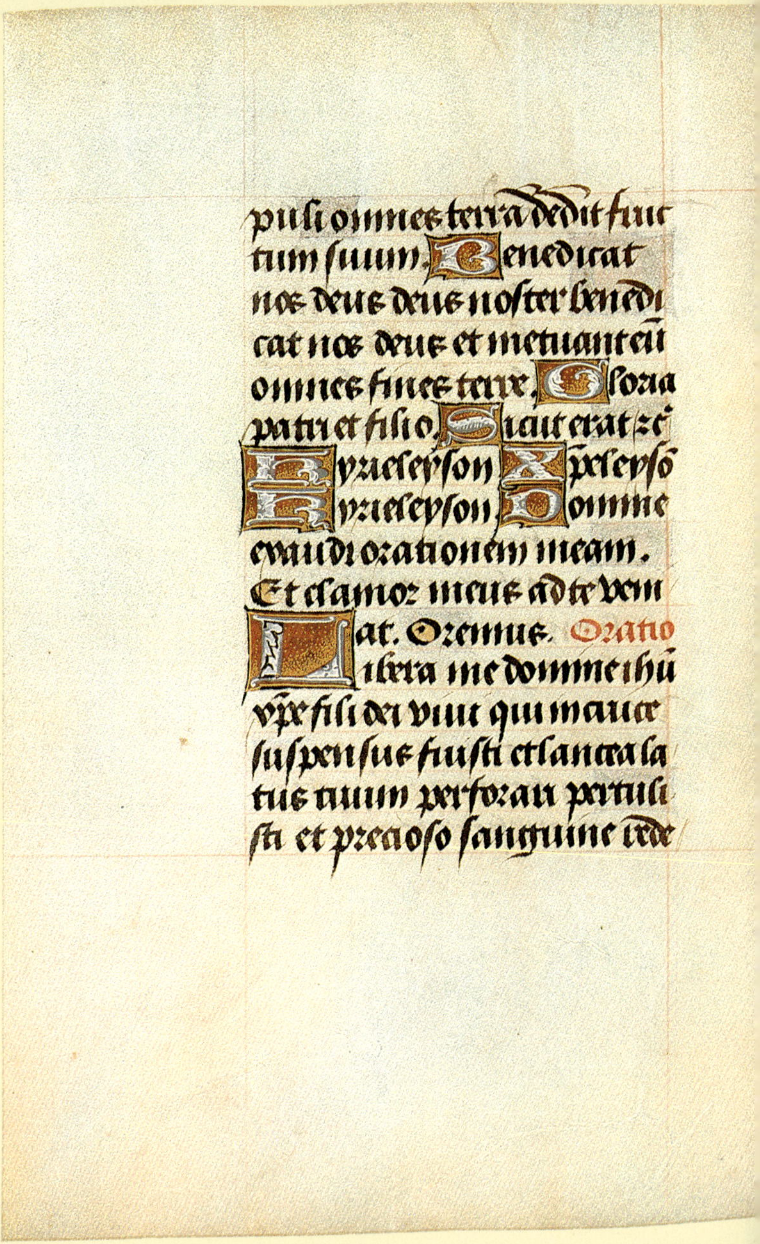

puli omnes terra dedit fruc
tum suum. Benedicat
nos deus deus noster benedi
cat nos deus et metuant eu
omnes fines terre. Gloria
patri et filio. Sicut erat zc
kyrieleyson Xpteleyso
kyrieleyson Domine
exaudi orationem meam.
Et clamor meus ad te veni
at. Oremus. Oratio
Libera me domine ihu
xpe fili dei viui qui manus
suspensus fuisti et lancea la
tus tuum perforari pertulis
sti et precioso sanguine rede

Deuota oro ad mariam virgi

Beata te
mina sca
maria ma
ter dei pie
tate plenis
sima sum
mi regis filia mater glorio
sissima . mater orphanorū
consolatio desolatorum. Uia
erranaum salus et spes in
te sperancium. Uirgo ante
partum. Uirgo in partu. et vir
go post partum. ffons mie
fons salutis et gratie. fons
pietatis et letitie. fons cōso

finem meum. O rex noster.

Et numerum dierum me-
orum quis est ut sciam quid
desit michi. O helioy.

Disrupisti domine vin-
cula mea tibi sacrificabo ho-
stiam laudis et nomen dm̄
inuocabo. O emanuel.

Deant fugia a me et nouē
qui requirat animam meā.

Clamaui O ypriste.
ad te domine dixi tu es spes
mea porcio mea in terra viuē-
cium. O affrox.

Hac mecum signum in bo-
no ut videant qui oderunt me

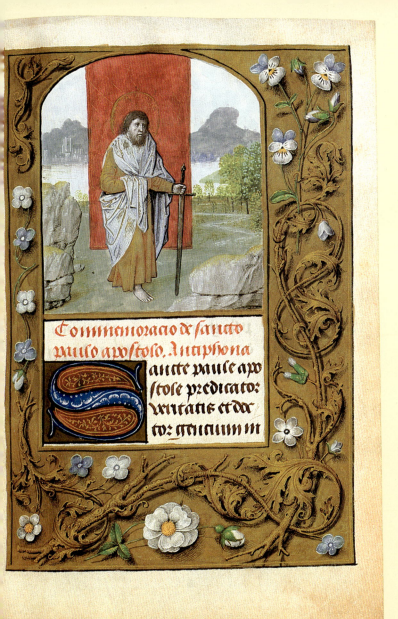

Commemoracio de sancto
paulo apostolo. Antiphona
ancte paule apo
stole predicato:
veritatis et do
cto: gencium in

tcirede ad dominum qui te
legit. ℣ Ora pro nobis sc̄e
paule. ℟ Vt digni efficiamur
promissione xp̄i. Oremus
Deus qui vniuersum
mundum sancti
pauli apostoli tui predicati
one docuisti da nobis q̄s.
Vt qui eius commemorati
onem agimus precibus eius
ipsa gradiamur. Per xp̄m
dominum nostrum Amen

38b

Commemoratio de sancto le
onardo. Antiphona.

Sanctae leonarde
confessor dei po
stula pro me
obsecro deum

omnipotentem. Vt purifiet a
nimam meam et corpus meum
ab omnibus peccatis libret
me ab omni tribulatione
et donet michi sic placere
deo omnibus diebus vite
mee. Vt pacem et tranquilli
tatem corporis et anime sa
nitatem habere merear in hoc
seculo et vitam eternam in
futuro. Amen

Memoria de sancto dauid
confessor. Antiphona

ste est qui ante
deum magnas
virtutes opa
tus est et omni-

terra doctrina eius repleta e
st. Intercedat pro peccatis
omnium populorum. Versus
Ora pro nobis sancte dauid
Responsum. Vt digni efficiamur
promissionibus xpi. Oremus

Deus qui beatum da
uid confessorem tuu
atq̃ pontificem angelo
nunciante triginta annis
anteq̃ nasceretur predixi
sti concede quesumus. vt
eius festiuitatem colimus
eius intercessione ad eter
na gaudia perueniamus
per xpm dominum nrm x

Memoria de sancto iseco
mmo. Antiphona.

Smisabo eum
vnv sapienti
qui edificauit
domum suam

z spū scō viuit et regnat dc̄ p.
altissime Oratio.

Omnipotens adorande
colende et tremende deus matt
ne adonay omniu beatitudi
nū et dignitatū mirabilis et
pius dispensator omniū dono
rum optimoz auctorq̄ vite lar
gissime erogatoz. Vt clementer
habundanter et permanenter di
gneris effundere sup me hodie
z cotidie multipley donū spūs
sancti gratie tue precor et pro
picius esto michi pctōz z da mi
victoriā cōtra dc̄ inimicoz meoz
visibilez z inuisibilez. P ppm.

De sancto iohanne baptista

Inter natos mulierum non surrexit maior iohanne baptista, qui viam domino preparauit in heremo. Xc. fuit homo missus a deo. R. Cui nomen erat iohannes. Dicmus. Oratio

Perpetuis nos quesumus domine beati iohannis baptiste tuere presidiis et quanto fragiliores sumus tanto magis necessariis attolle suffragiis. Per xpm dmm

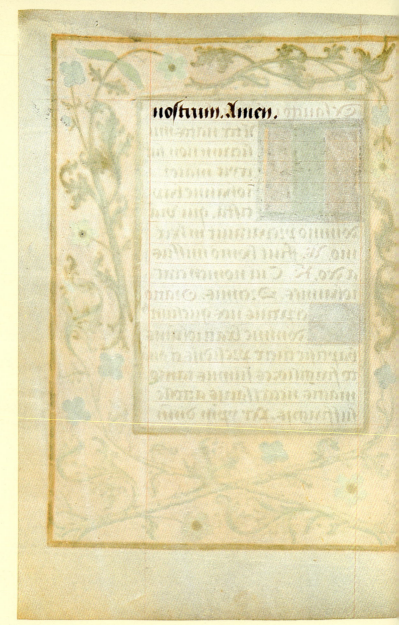

noſtrum. Amen.

martir ypi
adriane qui
ardendo me
ruisti fieri
quam plurii
um possessor premiorum. tu
pro nobis pater pie. roga re
gem vivine. ut post hec evisia
det nobis vera gaudia. ver.
Ora pro nobis beate martir
adriane. Ver. Ut digni efficia
mur promissione vpi sti.
Oremus. Oratio.
eus qui beatum adri
anum socios socios suos militi

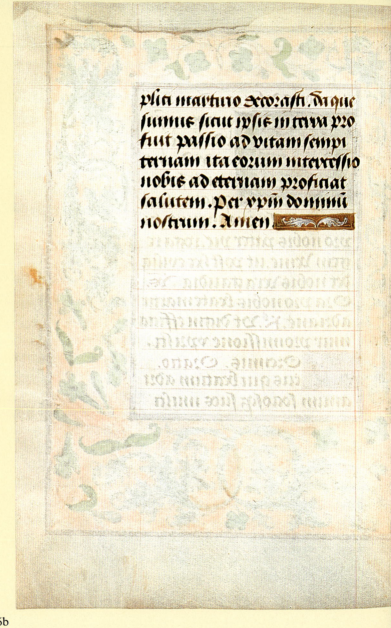

plia martirio decorasti. da que
summis sicut ipsis in terris pro
fuit passio ad vitam sempi
ternam ita eorum intercessio
nobis ad eternam proficiat
salutem. Per xpm dominum
nostrum. Amen

Memoria de sancto georgio.

Miles xpi glo
riose laus
syre tutor an
glie flecte gen
tis criminose
dura corda francie. fac discor
des gloriose. reduc concordie
ne sterniatur plebe clamose.
empta xpi sanguine. Vsue
Ora pro nobis beate martir
georgi. R. Vt digni efficia
mur promissione xpi. Oremus
cus qui nobis per bea
tum militem tuum
georgium sepe mirabiliter i

Memoria de sco ypoforo. ant

sancte ypofo
ir martir
ilxsu ypusti
qui pro cius
nomine pe
na pertulisti opem confer mi
serie atqz mundo tristi. qui
celestis glorie regna maiusta
ypofori sancti speciem quicui
qz tuetur illo nempe die nul
lo sanguore granetur. confer
solamen et mentis tolle gra
uamen. Judicis examen fac
mite sie omnibus. Vc Ora
pro nobis beate martir ypo

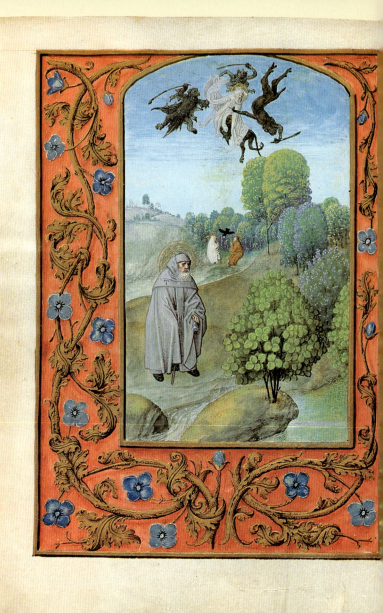

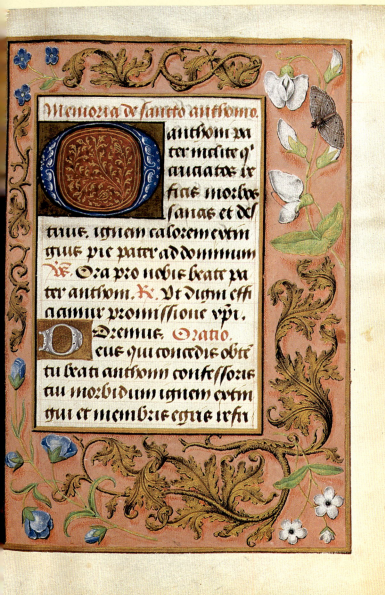

Memoria de sancto antsonio.

antsoni pa
ter inclite q'
auuato2 ic
ficit morbis
sanas et des
truis. ignem caloem extin
guis. pie pater ad dominium
V. Ora pro nobis beate pa
ter antsoni. R. Ut digni effi
ciamur promissione xpi.

Oremus. Oratio.

eus qui concedis obten
tu beati antsonii confessoris
tui morbidum ignem extin
gui et membris egnis resti

gratia prestare fac nos propia
us. ipsius martis et precib;
a vehementi ignis incendiis li
beratos integros mente et cor
pore tibi feliciter in gloria p
sentari. Per xpm dominum
nostrum. Amen

De sancto fabiano z sebastiano

secit dominus
vnum deple
be et clanta
tem visiose
eterne xdit
illis celebremus festuitatem
sancti sebastiani martire
gaudium sit in celo et in terra
pax hominibus bone volun
tatis. R. Letamini in domino
et exultate iusti. R. Et gloria
mini omnes recti corde. Oreq
E us qui beatos mar
tires tuos fabianum
et sebastianum virtute con

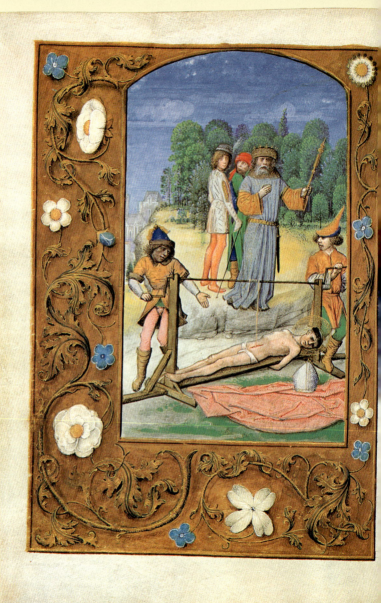

53b

memoria de sancto serasino.

Susape me sce
serasine intu
am fidem et
gratiam et con
serua me per
hos octo dies ab omni malo
et presta michi peragere ai
uua fide et omni prosperita
te et gratia finem bonum ui
te mee ut non proficiat mme
ulla mmicorum voluntatis
tibi ad laudem et honorem in
consolationem et gratiam ti
bi sancte serasine commendo
corpus meum et animam meam

54

Memoria de sancto thoma .x.

u per thome
sanguinem
quem pro te
impendit.
fac nos xpe
scandere quo thomas ascen
dit. R. Gloria et honore coro
nasti eum domine. K. Et con
stituisti eum super opera
manuum tuarum. Oracio
eus pro quo eccle
sia pontifex gloriosus
thomas martir gladiis im
piorum occubuit. presta
quesumus. Vt omnes qui

56

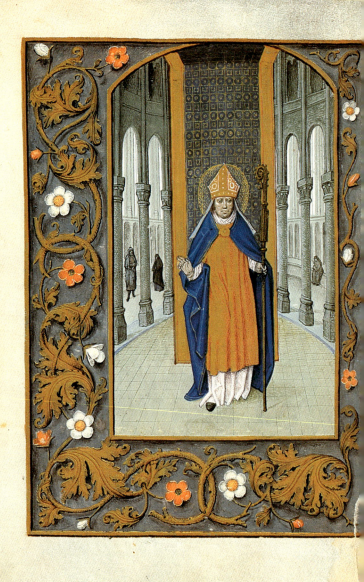

Memoria de sancto nicholao

B eatus nicho=
laus adhuc
puerulus
in multis iam
mo macera=
bat corpus.

V. Ora pro nobis beate pa
ter nicholae. R. Vt digni effi
ciamur promissione xpisti.
Oremus. Oratio.
Deus qui beatum nicho
laum gloriosum pontificem
tuum innumeris xcoruscasti
miraculis tribue nobis que=
sumus. Vt eius meritis et pre

59b

De beata Virgine maria. An.

S ub tuam pro
tectionem co
fugimus v
bi infirm ac
ceperunt vir
tutem et propter hoc tibi psal
lumus dei genitrix virgo. Ve
Post partum virgo inviola
ta permansisti. V. Dei gen
trix intercede pro nobis. Oro
oncede quesumus oro
miscricorde deus fragi
litati nostre presidium Vt q
sancte dei genitricis et virgin
nis marie memoriam agi

mus intcressione euis au
uisio a nostris iniquitatibz
resurgamus. Per ypm do
minum nostrum. Amen.

Memoria de sancta anna. ꝛ

O felix anna
cella mun
di culmine
lumen mun
di vna de
mentie sire
salutie porta leticie. nos dui
ne comenda gracie. Vs. Dif
fusa est gracia in labus tuis.
ꝛ. Propterea benedixit te de
us in eternum. Oremus. Or
Deus qui beatam annam
dilectissime genitricis
tue matrem egregiam odier
na die ad celestie uite suble

61

62b

Memoria de sancta margarita

E rat autem
margari
ta anno
quindum
cum ab im
pio osibrio
tradieturn in carterm. psue.
Ora pro nobis beata virgo
et martir margarita. K. Vt
digni effiaamur promissio
ne xpisti. Oremus. Oratio
Deus qui beatam mar
garitam virginem
et martirem tuam ad celos p
martiry palmam venire fe

Memoria de sancta elyzabeth.

A... nte thorū
quū conv-
gine fre-
quentate
nobis dul-
cia canti-
ca dragmatie. ℣. Diffusa est
gratia in labijs tuis. ℟.
Propterea benedixit te deus
in eternum. Oremus. oro.
          uorum corda fideliū
          deus miserator illu-
stra ut beate elyzabeth precibus gloriosis fac nos prospe-
ra mundi despicere et celesti

66b

Memoria de sancta sitha. an

Aue sancta
famula
sitha thu
vri. Que
cum tota
amina:
deo placuisti. Egenos et fie
biles de albo fouisti. Cecos
mutos debiles et claudos i
uisti. Semper elemosinam
dare quesiuisti. Deum et
ecclesiam vrgo dilexisti
ffraudem et nequiciam tu
mine odisti. Para nobis
gloriam quam tu merui

68b

Memoria de sancta katherina

Virgo sancta katherina generacionis gene-
ma vrbe alexandria costi regis erat filia. ℣. Ora pro nobis beata virgo et martir katherina. ℟. Vt digni efficiamur promissione xpi. Oremus eius qui dedisti legem moysi in summitate montis synai et in eodem loco per sanctos angelos tuos corpus beate katherine vir

70b

Memoria de sancta barbara.

Sancta bar-
bara pia
virgo qui
corporeū
dolorem
sustinui-
sti et deum exorasti. Vt quicū-
qz in honore te habernt in
omni vituperatione libera-
rentur te suppliciter exora-
mus. Vt deum pro nobis ex-
orare digneris quatinus
nos de mala infamia vicio
scandalo obprobrio impe-
dimento nimia paupertate

73b

Incipiunt hore beatissime
marie virginis secundum
usum sarum. Ad matutinas

Domine la
bia mea a
peries. Et
os meum
annunti
abit lau

dem tuam

Deus in adiutorium
meum intende. Dne
ad adiuuandum me festina
Gloria patri et filio et spi
ritui sancto. Sicut erat in
principio et nunc et semper

85b

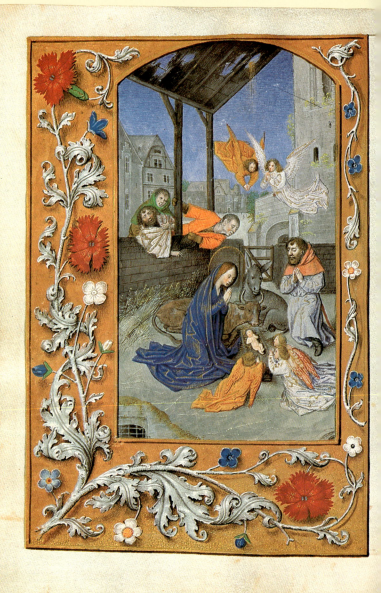

D ad vinam
Eus m ad
iutorium
meum in
tende. Do
mine ad
adiuuandum me festina.
Gloria patri et filio et
spiritu sancto Sicut erat
in principio et nunc et semp
et in secula seculorum amen
Uem arator spū vium
mentes tuorum vi
sita implse superna gratia
que tu arasti pectora
Memento salutis auc

℣. Gloriosa passio domini nostri Ihesu xpi perducat nos ad gaudia paradisi. ℟.

AD tertiam

DEus in adiutorium meum intende. Domine ad adiuuandum me festina.

Gloria patri. Hymnus.

Iam surgit hora tercia mentes tuorum visita in qua super crucis trophea gratia qua tu arasti pectora. Memento salutis auctor quod nostri

119b

Ad nonam
eus mad
iutorium
meum in
tende. Do
mine ad
adiuuandum me festina.
Gloria patri et filio. Item
Item arator spe mentes
tuorum visita imple
superna gracia que tu creasti
pectora. Memento salutis
auctor quod nostri quondam
corporis ex illibata virgi
na scendo formam sumpse
ris. Maria mater gracie

Ad vesperas

Deus in adiutorium meum intende. Domine ad adiuvandum me festina. Gloria patri et filio et spiritui sancto sicut erat in principio et nunc et semper et in secula seculorum amen. Alleluia. Post partum. Antiphona. Letatus sum in hiis que dicta sunt michi in domum domini ibimus. Antiphona. Stantes erant pedes nostri in atriis

Ad compl

Onuerte nos deus salutaris noster. Et auerte irā tuam a nobis

Deus madiutoriū meum intende. Domine ad adiuuandum me festia cōria patri et filio et spū sancto. Sicut erat in principio et nunc et semper et in secula seculorum amē raū. Cum icaiditate.

Isq̄quo domine obli

140

184b

Commendaciones animarū

Beati immaculati in via qui ambulant in lege domini. Beati qui scrutantur testimonia eius: in toto corde exquirunt eum. Non enim qui operantur iniquitatem in viis eius ambulaverunt. Tu mandasti mandata tua custodiri nimis. Utinam dirigantur viae meae: ad custodiendas iustificationes tuas.

Deus deus
meus respi
ce in me qr
me derelic
sti longe a
salute mea

Verba delictorum meorum
deus meus clamabo per
diem et non exaudies. et nocte
et non ad insipienciam michi
tu autem in sancto habi
tas laus israel. In te spera
uerunt patres nostri. spera
uerunt et liberasti eos. Ad
te clamauerunt et salui fa

265b

Incipiunt quindecim orationes domine ihesu xpe eterna dulcedo te amantium iubilus excedens omne gaudium et omne desiderium salus et amator peccatorum confitentium qui delicias tuas testatus es esse cum filys hominum propter hominem homo factus es in fine temporum. Memento omnis premeditationis et tuum meroris quem in hu

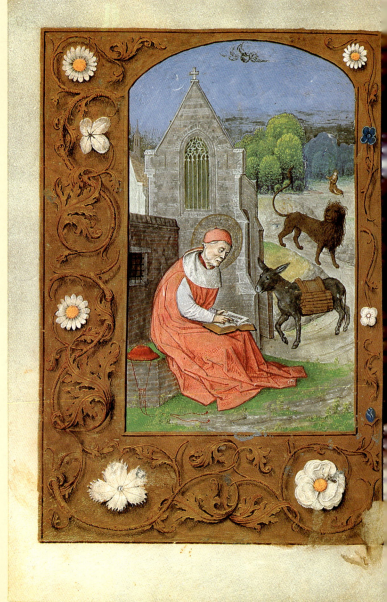

William, Lord Hastings

> *Woe, woe, for England! not a whit for me;*
> *For I, too fond, might have prevented this.*
> *Stanley did dream the boar did raze his helm;*
> *And I did scorn it, and disdained to fly.*
> *Three times to-day my foot-cloth horse did stumble,*
> *And startled when he looked upon the Tower,*
> *As loath to bear me to the slaughter-house.*
> *O! now I need the priest that spake to me:*
> *I now repent I told the pursuivant,*
> *As too triumphing how mine enemies*
> *To-day at Pomfret bloodily were butcher'd*
> *And I myself secure in grace and favour.*
> *O Margaret, Margaret! now thy heavy curse*
> *Is lighted on poor Hastings' wretched head.*

THUS speaks William, Lord Hastings, in Shakespeare's *King Richard III* when he has just been ordered to be executed by Richard, Duke of Gloucester, the future Richard III. Shakespeare's account of the event is derived from the *History of Richard III* by Sir Thomas More, the great scholar and statesman who was Henry VIII's first minister from 1529 to 1532, but who was disgraced and beheaded by that monarch in 1535 for his unflinching opposition to the breach with Rome. More was a small child when Hastings was beheaded on Friday, 13 June 1483, but he heard about what happened from another person who was present, John Morton, then bishop of Ely, who was to survive to become archbishop of Canterbury, lord chancellor, and a cardinal, dying in 1500. As a boy of twelve More had been sent to be educated in the archbishop's household. More's *Richard III* gives the traditional view of the king (younger brother of Edward IV) as the wicked uncle who murdered his two nephews, the boy-king Edward V and his brother Richard, Duke of York, who are known to history as the princes in the Tower. The traditional view of Richard III has been disputed, but the facts of Hastings' death are not in doubt. The Duke of Gloucester accused him of treason at a council in the Tower of London and he was forthwith taken out and executed. The Elizabethan chronicler and antiquary John Stow says in his *Annales of England*: 'So was he brought forth into the greene beside the chappell within the tower and his head laid downe upon a long log of timber and there stricken off and afterward his bodie with the head enterred at Winsore beside the bodie of king Edward.'

The destruction of Hastings was a signal act in the usurpation of the throne of England by Richard III. Richard himself is referred to as the boar in the speech from Shakespeare given above, for Richard's badge was a white boar. Stanley is Thomas, Lord Stanley, who was to be Earl of Derby in 1485 and who had married a sister of Hastings' wife. He was arrested and imprisoned on the fateful Friday the thirteenth – as was Bishop Morton – but managed to find favour with both Richard III and Henry VII, who overthrew Richard at the battle of Bosworth in 1485. The enemies who were butchered at Pomfret were Anthony Woodville, Earl Rivers, Edward V's maternal uncle; Richard Grey, Edward V's half-brother; and Sir Thomas Vaughan, who had been Edward V's chamberlain as prince of Wales. They were executed without trial at Pontefract Castle, in Yorkshire, though not in fact until twelve days after Hastings' death. They had been Hastings' enemies in that, at the court of Edward IV, after the English invasion of France in 1475, Hastings was the leader of a party which advocated friendship with Burgundy and Flanders in opposition to a party in favour of friendship with France, which was led by Edward IV's queen, Elizabeth Woodville, and her relations. Rivers was her eldest brother and Grey was her second son by her first marriage.

The Margaret whom the condemned Hastings apostrophizes is Margaret of Anjou, the queen of Henry VI, the last of the three Lancastrian kings of England. Henry ruled from 1423 to 1461 and was deposed by Edward IV, the first of the three Yorkist kings of England, in the Wars of the Roses. Margaret was the daughter of the artist and artistic Duke René of Anjou, titular King of Naples, Hungary, and Jerusalem. She married Henry VI in 1445 and bore him one child, in 1453, Edward, Prince of Wales. The prince was killed after the battle of Tewkesbury in 1471. According to Lancastrian legend he was brought before the victorious Edward IV, insulted by him, and murdered by the king's brothers, the Dukes of Clarence and Gloucester; Anthony, Earl Rivers; Thomas, Marquess of Dorset, Queen Elizabeth Woodville's eldest son by her first marriage; and William, Lord Hastings. The play *King Richard III* recounts Lancastrian legend: so in it Queen Margaret prays that none of Rivers, Dorset, and Hastings 'may live your natural age, But by some unlook'd accident cut off'. She is no more agreeable about Edward IV or Edward V, and decidedly outspoken about the Duke of Gloucester. Hastings remarks, 'My hair doth stand on end to hear her curses.' A more sober version of Henry VI and Margaret of Anjou's son's death is that he 'was taken fleeing to the townwards and slain in the field'.

William, Baron Hastings, for whom appears to have been made the book of hours which is the subject of this edition, was the close friend of King Edward IV, than whom he was some twelve years older. Edward was born on 28 April 1442: the exact date of William's birth is not known, but he was aged twenty-four and more at the time of his father's death on 20 October 1455. This father was Sir Leonard Hastings, owner of the manors of Kirby Muxloe in Leicestershire and Burton in Warwickshire. The Hastings family to which Sir Leonard belonged traced its origin to Robert, portreeve of Hastings in Sussex and steward to William the Conqueror. Robert's son William was steward to Henry II and the ancestor, through a younger son, of Sir Leonard Hastings.

Sir Leonard was a supporter of the Yorkist cause against the Lancastrians and well acquainted with the head of the Yorkists, Richard, Duke of York, father of Edward IV and Richard III, who was killed at the battle of Wakefield in 1460. Sir Leonard married into another not quite so ancient family, that of Camoys. His bride was Alice, daughter of Thomas, Lord Camoys, and by her he had four sons, William, Richard, Ralph, and Thomas, and two daughters who are known, Elizabeth and Anne. Richard, Ralph, and Thomas seem to have passed their lives largely as agents and aiders of William, although Richard became Baron Welles as a result of marrying the heiress of the Lords Welles. Elizabeth was the wife of Sir John Donne, who was knighted at the battle of Tewkesbury in 1471. Elizabeth and John were married probably in 1465. He died in 1503, she in 1508. Anne Hastings married into the family of the Barons Ferrers, of Groby, in Leicestershire.

Sir Leonard Hastings probably regarded himself as having had a useful life, but he never achieved success on the national, and international, scale remotely like that won by his eldest son. This is evidenced by the difference in length and detail of his will and his son's. Sir Leonard's, made on 8 October 1455, twelve days before he died, is a relatively simple document. William's, made twenty-six years later, is prolix, and so is his wife's, which was drawn in 1503.

William began his career in his father's footsteps. In 1455–56 he was sheriff of Warwickshire and Leicestershire, as Sir Leonard had been in 1454. On 23 April 1456 the Duke of York, at his castle of Fotheringay, in Northamptonshire, granted William an annuity on condition that he should serve the duke 'above all others, and attend him at all times, (his allegiance to the king excepted)'. William became one of the inner circle of Yorkists, and when on 12 October 1459 the Yorkists and Lancastrians clashed at Ludford bridge, in front of Ludlow castle in Shropshire, he was present on the Yorkist side.

Ludford was a disaster for the Yorkists. The Duke of York, with his second son, Edmund, Earl of Rutland, fled through Wales to Ireland, of which he was governor (in official parlance, lieutenant). The future Edward IV, at the time Earl of March, went with his maternal uncle Richard Neville, Earl of Salisbury, and Salisbury's son, Richard, Earl of Warwick, to Devonshire and across the channel to Calais, an English possession of which Warwick was captain or governor. Warwick is that Warwick who is known to English history as 'the kingmaker', and the Nevilles were one of the most powerful families in England. Cecily Neville, Salisbury's sister, was York's wife. The Nevilles belonged to the Yorkist party. Their rivals, the Percy family, supported Henry VI, or more directly Queen Margaret, who ruled for her husband, who, though of undoubted piety, was simple in the ways of the world.

The Yorkists left behind at Ludlow, who included William Hastings, surrendered to the Lancastrians, who were led by the king and the queen. Margaret duly summoned a parliament, at

Coventry, to consolidate her victory, at which the Yorkists were attainted. Hastings, like others, was condemned to lose his lands, but, like others, he was allowed to buy them back and obtain a pardon.

In 1460 the Yorkists returned. Salisbury, Warwick and March landed in Kent and captured the person of King Henry VI at the battle of Northampton on 10 July. In September the Duke of York landed near Chester from Ireland and in parliament in London laid claim to the throne. He was adjudged heir apparent on 9 November, Edward, Prince of Wales, the son of Henry VI and Margaret of Anjou, thus being disinherited.

Margaret was unlikely to accept this, nor did she. She mustered her supporters, and on 30 December 1460 the Lancastrians fell on the Duke of York and various of his family and friends, who were keeping Christmas at the duke's castle of Sandal, near Wakefield, in Yorkshire. York and Rutland were killed, and Salisbury was taken to Pontefract Castle and beheaded on the following morning. Edward, Earl of March, was in the west country, at Ludlow Castle and Shrewsbury. He advanced with an army to join Warwick, who was in possession of London and the king. William Hastings was with Edward, and on 2 February 1461 the young Duke of York defeated a Lancastrian force at Mortimer's Cross, near Wigmore, in Herefordshire. In the meantime, Queen Margaret, her strength increased by Scottish auxiliaries, was descending on the capital. On 17 February she defeated Warwick at St Albans, and Henry VI was able to rejoin his wife and son.

Warwick had now lost the king, so he made another. He joined forces with Edward of York, and on 27 February the two of them entered London. On 4 March Edward was proclaimed king, the fourth of that name. He had to fight for his crown. The decisive engagement was at Towton, not far from Pontefract, on 29 March. Afterwards, on the field of battle, the new king dubbed six knights. The first of them was William Hastings.

Edward IV was crowned in Westminster Abbey on Sunday, 28 June 1461. At the festivities the king's two surviving brothers George and Richard were made Dukes of Clarence and Gloucester, and ten peers were created: two earls and eight barons. Hastings was one of the barons. Right from the start of the reign he was at the centre of affairs and throughout it he held the two important offices of chamberlain of the royal household and master of the mint. As chamberlain he was overseer of the king's establishment, with considerable patronage at his disposal, and master of state occasions. As master of the mint he was responsible for the manufacture of coinage, under a contract with the crown.

It is probable that Edward IV saw in William Hastings a counterforce to Richard Neville, Earl of Warwick. Warwick was the kingmaker: Hastings was the king's creation. The list of his appointments is long. It includes the governorship of many castles: Leicester (1461), Higham Ferrers, in Northamptonshire (1461). Castle Donington, in Leicestershire (1461), Oakham, in Rutland (1461), Rockingham, in Northamptonshire (1462), Northampton (1462), Harlech, in North Wales (1464), Huntingdon (1464), Fotheringay (1469), Beaumaris, in Anglesey, North Wales (1469), Nottingham (1471), Newcastle-under-Lyme, in Shropshire (1474), Tutbury, in Staffordshire (1474), Sheffield (1474), Peveril, or the Peak, in Derbyshire (1474). Rockingham and Northampton Hastings held jointly with his brother Ralph. Also, on 8 May 1461, William Hastings had been made receiver-general of the royal duchy of Cornwall, and on 31 July the same year he became chamberlain of North Wales. Both grants were for life. On 21 March 1462 he received the great honour of being named a knight of the Garter, and by that date he had made a splendid marriage. Probably early in 1462, he married a sister of the kingmaker. Presumably King Edward IV himself had a hand in the match.

Richard Neville, Earl of Warwick, had three brothers and six sisters. The brothers were Thomas, John, and George. Thomas and John were made knights of the Bath in 1449, but Thomas was killed at the battle of Wakefield. John had been chamberlain of the royal household in the last months of Henry VI's reign, and Edward IV made him Baron Montagu in 1461 and a knight of the Garter in 1462. In 1464 he defeated the Lancastrian resistance at the battles of Hedgeley Moor and Hexham, in Northumberland, and as a reward received the earldom of Northumberland, traditionally held by the Nevilles' enemies, the Percies. However, in 1469 Henry Percy, who had been Earl of Northumberland, made peace with the king and regained his title. John Montagu was compensated by being made Marquess of Montagu. He was to join his eldest brother Warwick in rebellion against Edward IV, and like him was killed at the battle of Barnet in 1471. George Neville was a churchman. Privilege surrounded his early career, and in 1458, at the age of twenty-seven, he was consecrated bishop of Exeter. Two years later he was lord chancellor. He remained such under Edward IV until 1467. By this time he had become archbishop of York, in 1465. During the brief restoration of Henry VI in 1470 to 1471 he was chancellor again. He submitted to Edward IV when the Yorkist king was restored in 1471 and thought himself high in favour once more, but in April 1472 he was arrested and spent two years in prison in the castle of Hammes, near Calais, which was under the command of Hastings. The archbishop died in 1476.

The Neville sisters were Joan, Cicely, Alice, Eleanor, Katharine, and Margaret. Three of them became countesses, and one was briefly a duchess. Joan's husband was William FitzAlan, Earl of Arundel. Cicely married twice: first, Henry, the last of the Earls of Warwick of the Beauchamp family, who was made Duke of Warwick in 1445 and died the following year, aged twenty-one; and secondly, John Tiptoft, the intellectual and travelled Earl of Worcester. Alice was the wife of Henry, Lord Fitzhugh. Eleanor married Thomas, Lord Stanley, the future Earl of Derby. Margaret was Countess of Oxford through marrying John de Vere, Earl of Oxford.

Katharine, the fifth girl, had two husbands. Her first, whom she married in 1458, or shortly before, was William Bonville, who became Lord Harington on the death of his maternal grandfather in March that year. William Bonville's father and father's father were also called William. The grandfather, Lord Bonville, saw both his son and eighteen-year-old grandson slain at the battle of Wakefield in 1460 and he himself was beheaded on the day after the battle of St Albans, 18 February 1461, by order of Margaret of Anjou. William Bonville, Lord Harington, and Katherine Neville had a daughter Cecily who succeeded her father in the barony of Harington and her great-grandfather in that of Bonville. Her mother, Katharine, married as her second husband William, Lord Hastings. They had four sons, Edward, Richard, William, and George, and one daughter, Anne.

Hastings was employed by Edward IV both as a soldier and a

diplomat. After the triumph of the Yorkists in 1461, Margaret of Anjou went to Scotland and thence to France, where she obtained help from her cousin, King Louis XI. In autumn 1462 she returned by way of Scotland to the north of England and established herself at the castles of Bamburgh, Dunstaburgh, and Alnwick there. An expedition against these strongholds was led by Warwick, the king being prevented by an attack of measles from being present himself, and Hastings was one of the commanders. From the campaign there survives a letter home from the Norfolk gentleman John Paston *minor*. In it he claims good acquaintance with 'my Lord Hastings and my Lord Dacre which be now greatest about the King's person'. Dacre was intimate with Edward IV, but never achieved political position. Hastings' friendship with the king was such that he was almost certainly one of the few people in the secret of Edward's marriage.

Various royal ladies were considered as queens for England, and the Earl of Warwick was active in the quest. Mary of Guelders, the widowed Queen of Scotland, Bona of Savoy, the sister-in-law of Louis XI of France, and Isabella, the future Queen of Castile, were all candidates, but Edward's choice was to fall on an English widow some years his senior. This was Elizabeth, daughter of Richard Woodville, Earl Rivers, and Jacquetta of Luxembourg, widow of John, Duke of Bedford, the brother of King Henry V. Elizabeth's first husband was Sir John Grey, a Leicestershire knight, who was killed at the battle of St Albans in 1461.

On 13 April 1464 Dame Elizabeth Grey and William, Lord Hastings, made an agreement for a marriage between their families. Elizabeth's elder son, Thomas, or, in the case of his death, his brother Richard, should wed the eldest daughter to be born within the next five or six years to Hastings. If no such daughter were available, then the bride should be a daughter born within the same period to William's brother Ralph; or, failing such a daughter, one of the daughters of William's sister Anne Ferrers. If certain lands which had belonged to a Sir William Asteley or had been part of the inheritance of Dame Elizabeth were recovered in the title or right of Thomas or Richard, then Elizabeth and Hastings would share the rents of them by halves while Thomas Grey, or if he died, Richard Grey, were under

96

twelve. Hastings was to pay Elizabeth five hundred marks for the marriage, but if it did not take place, she would pay him two hundred and fifty marks. The marriage did not come about, but Thomas Grey, who became Marquess of Dorset, married as his second wife Cecily Bonville, Hastings' stepdaughter, in 1474. He was then twenty-four and she was thirteen.

Eighteen days after Elizabeth Grey and William Hastings signed their family alliance, Elizabeth secretly married the King of England. Hastings' manor of Kirby Muxloe may have been one of the places of their honeymoon.

From 1464 to the time of Warwick's attempt to restore the Lancastrians in 1470, Hastings was employed on a number of diplomatic missions. In 1464 he was joined with Warwick and his brother Northumberland to make a truce with Scotland. In March 1465 Warwick and Hastings were treating with representatives of Charles, Count of Charolais, the heir to the duchy of Burgundy, known to history as Charles 'the Bold'. Hastings was already in receipt of a pension from Charles, a thousand crowns a year, granted to him on 4 May 1461. In May 1465 there was a project for a conference between representatives of the duchies of Burgundy and Brittany and the kingdoms of England and France. The English representatives were headed by Warwick and Hastings, but the conference came to nothing because of a revolt against Louis XI of France. The year 1466 saw Hastings and others discussing with Burgundy commercial relations and marriages between Charolais and Edward IV's sister Margaret, and between the Duke of Clarence and Charolais's daughter Mary. The idea of a marriage between Charolais and Margaret of York was pursued the following year, when he became Duke of Burgundy. Hastings was again one of the negotiators, and the wedding took place in 1468.

Edward IV was no puppet king, and a rupture between him and the Earl of Warwick was inevitable. Warwick thought to promote an alternative king in George, Duke of Clarence, whom he married to his elder daughter Isobel, but Clarence was plainly unsuitable, so Warwick decided he must restore Henry VI, who was being held in the Tower. This necessitated reconciliation with Margaret of Anjou, who was living with her son in France. Louis XI could be trusted to use his best offices towards such an end, and in May 1470 Warwick arrived in France, having broken openly with Edward IV. On 13 September he and his forces landed in the west of England to restore the Lancastrians. A hard-won friendship with Queen Margaret had been secured by arranging a marriage between her son and Warwick's younger daughter, Anne. The desertion of Warwick's brother John Neville, Marquess of Montagu, was decisive against Edward, and at the end of the month he, with Gloucester, Hastings, Rivers, and a few other faithful, sailed from King's Lynn, in Norfolk, to Holland, which was a Burgundian province. On the way they were chased by ships belonging to the association of north German mercantile towns called the Hanseatic League. The League were at war with England as a result of a lost lawsuit.

The fugitives took refuge with the governor of Holland, Louis, Lord of Gruuthuse, with whom Edward stayed at his residences at the Hague from 9 October to 26 December 1470 and Bruges from 13 January to 19 February 1471. Gruuthuse's house at Bruges is now the museum of that name there. Gruuthuse was chamberlain to the Duke of Burgundy and had been employed by him to further Yorkist interests at the court of Scotland in 1460 to 1461. In 1466 to 1467 he was a joint ambassador to England. In June 1467 he took part in London in a tournament staged between Anthony Woodville and Antoine, the Bastard of Burgundy, eldest of the illegitimate sons of Philip 'the Good', Duke of Burgundy 1419–67.

Louis of Gruuthuse was a considerable patron of the arts, and there survive one hundred and sixty-two manuscripts from his library, of which a hundred and forty-two are in the Bibliothèque Nationale, Paris. He was collecting them over some thirty years, *circa* 1460–90, and whilst most date from this period, forty are older material which Gruuthuse acquired, such as the collection of Middle Dutch verse from the second half of the fourteenth century, which is known as the Gruuthuse manuscript and belongs to Baron Ernest Van Caloen, at the castle of Ten Berghe at Bruges. The books in which Gruuthuse was principally interested were ones on history. Next came devotional texts and afterwards romances of chivalry. The later years during which he was active as a collector saw the development and establishment of what is called the Ghent-Bruges school of manuscript illumination, from the two Flemish cities where it was centred. The book of hours of William, Lord Hastings, in the British Library is the earliest surviving masterpiece of the Ghent-Bruges school.

Louis of Gruuthuse deserves pious remembrance by all visitors to the British Library, because one of the foundation collections of the Library is the old royal library of England, in effect begun by Edward IV, and Edward seems to have been mainly inspired to acquire books by the example of Gruuthuse. There may well be a reminiscence of this in the presentation miniature in Edward IV's copy of volume I of Jean de Wavrin's Chronicles of England, now Royal MS. 15 E. iv in the Department of Manuscripts of the British Library (f. 14). This shows Edward, seated, receiving the book from a kneeling man. In the room are four other people, in two pairs; one of these people is certainly, and another probably, wearing the emblem of the order of the Garter, namely a dark blue velvet garter, bearing in letters of gold the motto 'HONI SOIT QUI MAL Y PENSE', on his left leg below the knee. The four people may be the Duke of Gloucester, Lord Hastings, Earl Rivers, and Gruuthuse.

Edward IV was never a bibliophile like Louis of Gruuthuse, and the size of the first royal library of England compares poorly with that of the royal library of France at the end of the fourteenth century, which numbered some thousand manuscripts, or that of the ducal library of Burgundy under Philip 'the Good', who owned around nine hundred. The best description of Edward's books remains that of J.P. Gilson, Keeper of the Department of Manuscripts of the British Museum – now the Department of Manuscripts of the Reference Division of the British Library – from 1911 to 1929, in the *Catalogue of Western Manuscripts in the Old Royal and King's Collections*, which appeared over his name and that of Sir George F. Warner, his predecessor as Keeper of Manuscripts, in 1921:

'The Ghent and Bruges illuminators evidently catered for a class that wished to be read to, rather than to read. Their productions give the impression of being bought by the pound, or rather by the hundredweight. These huge volumes are not to be handled. They are to be placed on a high desk and read aloud by a standing lector, over whose shoulder the noble master or mistress may occasionally take a glance at a miniature, without inspecting it too closely in detail; for these pictures look better at a little distance, and reproductions of them are most effective when executed on a smaller scale. The language is almost exclusively French. As to contents, it is equally clear that they tend to entertainment and edification rather than study and the advancement of learning. History there is in plenty, but chiefly of the kind that is read for example of noble deeds, and shades off imperceptibly into historical romance.'

One book similar in format and content to those of Edward IV survives which apparently belonged to William, Lord Hastings. This is a copy of volume II of the Chronicles of France and England by the French historian Jean Froissart, who lived from 1338 to perhaps 1410. It is Royal MS. 18 E. i in the British Library and was written and illuminated *circa* 1480. At the beginning (f. 12) it has a miniature of Philip 'the Bold', Duke of Burgundy 1363 to 1404, returning from a military expedition. Associated with the miniature is an ornamental border, in the centre of the bottom of which are the arms and crest of Hastings, in outline, over which some zealous person has placed a stamp of ownership of the British Museum in red. Hastings' arms, with their colours, were 'argent, a maunch sable', that is, a black sleeve on a silver shield. His crest was 'out of a coronet, composed of four large and four small fleurs de lis, or, a bull's head sable', a black bull's head rising out of a gold coronet.

Back in England the winter of 1470 to 1471 saw Henry VI nominally in power and the Earl of Warwick really so. Margaret of Anjou and her son lingered in France, and the King of France, Louis XI, busied himself in urging the now dependent English government to aid him in his schemes against the Duke of Burgundy. This spurred Duke Charles to assist his brother-in-law of England; they met early in January 1471, and on 11 March Edward, Gloucester, Rivers, and Hastings, with some twelve hundred mercenary soldiers, set sail to reconquer England. They landed in Yorkshire and marched south. Their reception was lukewarm, but the adherence of Sir William Stanley, brother of Thomas, the future Earl of Derby, and a reconciliation with the Duke of Clarence, in which Hastings played a part, altered matters. Edward entered London on 11 April, and Archbishop George Neville, who was in charge there, thought it prudent to hand over Henry VI to him. Warwick was hard behind, and on 13 April, Easter eve, Edward marched back northwards to meet him.

They fought at Barnet, eleven miles north of London, early on Easter morning, 14 April 1471. Edward's army was commanded by himself, Clarence, Gloucester, Rivers, and Hastings; Warwick's by himself, his brother the Marquess of Montagu, and his brother-in-law the Earl of Oxford. Warwick was defeated, and he and Montagu were killed. Edward IV was able to get back to London in time for a combined Easter and thanksgiving service at St Paul's.

However, Queen Margaret and her son remained. They had landed at Weymouth, in Dorset, on the afternoon of 13 April. Lancastrians and Yorkists advanced towards each other. They met at Tewkesbury, in Gloucestershire, on 4 May. The king commanded the centre of his army, Gloucester the left, and Hastings the right. The engagement resulted in the defeat of the Lancastrians, the capture of their queen, and the death of their Prince of Wales.

As governor of Calais Warwick had held a key position of command over the narrow seas between England and the continent. This command needed to be in the hands of a more loyal, and a lesser, man. It went to Hastings, but his appointment, on 17 July 1471, was as lieutenant, not captain of Calais. He took his duties very seriously. Calais was a place in daily communication with the Low Countries, where two books of hours were apparently made for Hastings: the one at present under discussion and one in the Fundación Lázaro-Galdiano in Madrid, Inv. nr. 15503.

In the autumn of 1472 Louis de la Gruuthuse came to England to be fêted and rewarded for his friendship in adversity. Hastings, as chamberlain of the royal household, played a lead in the happenings. Gruuthuse and he took a ceremonial bath together at Windsor castle, 'and when they had been in their baths as long as was their pleasure, they had green ginger, diverse syrups, comfits, and hippocras'. On 13 October Gruuthuse was made Earl of Winchester, with an annuity of £200.

Burgundian help in 1470 to 1471 had to be paid for in more real terms, however, and in the summer of 1475 Edward IV invaded France. It is doubtful whether he ever intended more than a demonstration, and on 29 August the Kings of France and England had a summit meeting on the bridge of Picquigny on the Somme, some six miles north-west of Amiens. The scene is depicted on a misericord under the seat of the sovereign's stall in St George's chapel, Windsor castle, of which Edward IV began the rebuilding in 1475 and where he and Hastings were to be buried. Security precautions were elaborate, for nobody had forgotten the assassination of Duke John 'the Fearless' of Burgundy at a conference on a bridge in 1419.

Edward IV's suite included Hastings and Louis XI's Philippe de Commines, whose memoirs have earned him the title of the father of modern history. Commines knew Hastings well and describes him as 'a person of singular wisdom and virtue, in great authority with his master, and not without cause, having ever served him faithfully'.

Edward IV's French expedition resulted in a treaty between France and England which was financially advantageous to Edward and a number of his advisers, including Hastings. Hastings was very reluctant to be indebted to the King of France, and Commines, who, when he was in the service of Burgundy, had been the intermediary for Hastings' receiving his Burgundian pension in 1461, was entrusted with the task of overcoming his scruples. Commines wrote several letters to Hastings, and finally Louis sent Pierre Claret, his chief steward, to England with two thousand gold crowns, twice the amount of the Burgundian pension. Claret was under strict orders to get a receipt from Hastings, since Louis wanted it on record which of the great in England were in his pay.

Hastings and Claret had a private interview in London, without anybody else present. Hastings took the money, but refused to sign anything for it. Claret besought Hastings for at least a letter of three lines addressed to the King of France, so that Louis would not think Claret had stolen the money. Hastings agreed that Claret was not being unreasonable, but continued: 'This gift comes from the good will of the king your master, not at at my request. If you want me to take it, put it here in my sleeve, but there will be no letter or witness. I do not want it said that the chamberlain of England is the pensioner of the King of France and that my receipts are to be found in his exchequer.'

Claret had to return to France empty-handed, at which Louis was very cross. Nevertheless, Louis recognized a worthy adversary, and Hastings' French pension was continued without his ever having to give a receipt for it. His obstinacy also stood him in good stead with the Duke of Burgundy. The Milanese ambassador, Panicharola, reported to the Duke of Milan in 1476 that the Duke of Burgundy was very friendly towards Hastings and did not regard him as bought by the King of France.

Commines says that Claret and Hastings had their meeting in Hastings' room, in London. This could have been an official room of the chamberlain in a royal residence or a room in a private dwelling of Hastings. He is recorded to have leased a house in London, on 20 June 1463, from the prior of the Augustinian canons of St Bartholomew's, West Smithfield, London. It was situated by St Paul's Wharf, the quay for St Paul's cathedral, on the Thames, and measured twenty-four feet from east to west. There was a yard to the north of the house and another piece of land, five feet broad from east to west, which was part of a building where dyeing took place. Hastings' house had two 'solars', or upstairs living rooms, and the lease was for sixty years from 24 June 1463, at a rent of one red rose a year, if demanded. If the occupation lasted beyond sixty years the rent became 10s. a year.

Outside London Hastings' chief residences were the paternal manor of Kirby Muxloe and the manor of Ashby-de-la-Zouch, also in Leicestershire, which the king gave him in 1464. Both places he was allowed to fortify, being given the royal licence necessary, for Kirby in 1464 and for Ashby in 1473. Accounts survive of construction work done between 1480 and 1484 at Kirby Muxloe, and are Egerton MS. 3136 in the Department of Manuscripts at the British Library. The master masons were John Cowper, a native of Tattershall, in Lincolnshire, and Robert Stainforth, his assistant. Kirby Muxloe was rebuilt as a true castle with a moat, on the lines of a traditional mediaeval English castle. The building material, however, was brick, and the gun-ports are amongst the earliest in England. At Ashby-de-la-Zouch Hastings made several additions, including an impressive keep, which was as much a self-contained stronghold as the castle keeps of earlier days, with a large hall, living rooms, bed rooms, kitchen, cellars, and the like. Other improvements include a chapel.

King Edward IV of England died on Wednesday, 9 April 1483, just under forty-one years of age. His health had been failing for about a year, and in the summer of 1482 Hastings, when presumably on his way to or from Calais, had told the mayor of Canterbury that the king might not last long and that political upheavals might be expected. Hastings was now on very bad terms with the queen, Elizabeth Woodville, who had wanted the governorship of Calais for her brother, Anthony, Earl Rivers, and the court was split by a feud between Hastings and Thomas, Marquess of Dorset, the queen's elder son by her first marriage, who had married Hastings' stepdaughter Cecily. Gossip among the French and Italians living in London had it that Dorset and Hastings had quarrelled over a woman, said to be the king's mistress Jane Shore.

Edward IV's heir was a boy of twelve, Edward V, who was living at Ludlow Castle under the care of his uncle Rivers. A struggle for power was inevitable, and Hastings was the potential kingmaker. His loyalty to the memory of Edward IV was unwavering, and he regarded the Woodvilles as a danger to the realm. When there was discussion about the size of the force by which the new king should be accompanied to London, Hastings threatened to retire to Calais if there were no limits set on the army the Woodvilles might muster for this purpose. He opposed any idea that the queen might become regent and preferred a regency council presided over by the Duke of Gloucester, Edward IV's sole surviving brother. The thirty-year-old Gloucester was declared protector of England, and Hastings proudly exclaimed that the government had been transferred from the queen's blood to the old blood royal, and that without one drop of blood having been shed on either side. Too late he discovered the true foe and tried to make peace with the queen. By the end of June the Duke of Gloucester was King Richard III, and Hastings and the leaders of the queen's party were all dead or in exile. It was undoubtedly the division between Hastings and the Woodvilles which allowed Richard III to seize the throne.

To the calculating man who was Richard III, Hastings' death was a political expediency. Hastings and Rivers had long been the two most popular men in England, so there had to be some explanations to the public. A proclamation was made in London to the effect that Hastings had been conspiring to assassinate Gloucester and take over the government; that he had enticed Edward IV into debauchery and thus shortened his days; and that since Edward had died Hastings had been living in sin with Jane Shore. It does appear that Jane Shore had been living under Hastings' protection since the death of Edward IV; there was propaganda about witchcraft by her, and the queen, and she was made to do public penance for her loose ways. However, Richard III was not vindictive. He allowed Hastings' body to be buried in St George's Chapel, Windsor Castle, next to Edward IV's, as Hastings had wished and Edward had granted. Katharine, Lady Hastings, put up a chantry chapel over the tomb, which still stands in the north choir aisle of St George's. It was dedicated to St Stephen, the first martyr, and contains wall paintings of the story of the saint. There is a fine stone screen.

Hastings had made a will on 27 June 1481. It was much concerned with the welfare of his soul and taking heaven by storm. For the expenses of his burying and tomb he left 100 marks. A mark was worth 13s. 4d. Twenty pounds 'of lawful money of England' were to be given to the 'minister of divine service and funeral observances the day of burying', to those of the pensioners known as the Poor Knights of Windsor who were present on the day, and in other 'deeds of alms' at the discretion of the executors. To the dean and canons of St George's, Windsor, Hastings bequeathed a jewel of gold or silver, worth £20, in remembrance, and lands to the value of £20 a year, so that there should always be a priest to say mass and divine service daily 'at the altar next to the place where my body shall be buried . . . and there to pray daily for the king's prosperous estate during his life and after his death for his soul, for the souls of me, my wife, and for all Christian souls'.

The Hastings family tombs were at the Premonstratensian abbey of Sulby, in Northamptonshire, and to Sulby were left £40, vestments, and plate, lands to the value of 5 marks a year, and two advowsons. In return the abbot and canons of Sulby were to celebrate a solemn annual requiem for the souls of Hastings, his wife, 'mine ancestors there lying specially, with all other my ancestors and all Christian souls', and there was to be a daily requiem mass by a priest of the abbey for the Hastings dead and 'every priest of the abbey saying mass in the said abbey daily for ever say an especial collect in every of their masses for my soul and all the souls before rehearsed'. Sulby was not a large abbey. It averaged ten inmates, including novices, at the time of Hastings' death. On the occasion of Hastings' death his executors were to arrange for a thousand priests each to say the office and mass of the dead, preferably all on the same day. Each priest was to have 6*d*. for his trouble.

A hundred pounds were to be divided among the poor and the friars of Nottingham, Northampton, Leicester, and Derby. There were bequests, for prayers for Hastings and his dead, to the abbey of Augustinian canons at Leicester, to the Franciscan friars at Leicester and one other house of friars there, to every parish church in Leicester and to Newark hospital at Leicester. Hastings' executors were to rebuild the chapel on the bridge at Leicester with £100 and endow a priest to say mass daily there for seven years. The parish church of Ashby-de-la-Zouch got vestments and an altar cloth, together worth 100*s*., and £50 to find a priest to say daily, 'for me and the souls afore rehearsed', mass and other prayers. Hastings' other testamentary provisions were about money and property, including the marriage of his daughter Anne to George, Earl of Shrewsbury, who had been made Hastings' ward.

Twenty years after her husband's execution, Katharine, Lady Hastings, 'having perfect memory and whole mind, considering that nothing is more certain than death, and therefore at all times willing to be ready unto death, and to look for the time of the coming of the same, whereunto it is required, not only disposition ghostly, but also of such goods as God of his unmeasurable goodness hath lent me the use and exercise of', made her will, on 22 November 1503.

It is more personal than William's. She was to be buried in the lady chapel of the parish church of Ashby-de-la-Zouch. 'I will that a priest be found to sing in the said chapel for my father, and my lady my mother, my lord my husband's souls, and in special for those souls which I am most bounden to cause to be prayed for, the space of three years next ensuing, after my departing, and if my priest Sir William Englondel be contented to pray for me in the said place, and for the above said, then I will that he be admitted to the said service before any other priest.'

The lady chapel at Ashby got a set of vestments of baudekin, red and green, 'my little gilded chalice', a printed mass book, and a printed breviary. Baudekin was a rich embroidered material, originally made with a warp of gold thread and a woof of silk. Ashby church itself received seven surplices, whilst a missal covered with red velvet was to be given to a poor church at the direction of Katharine's executors. A yearly memorial was founded at Newark hospital, Leicester. Katharine had some debts to her daughter by her first marriage, Cecily, Marchioness of Dorset, which were to be paid with a bed of arras, with its canopy and counterpane, 'which she late borrowed of me', a tablet of gold, 'that she now hath in her hands for a pledge', four curtains of blue sarsenet, three cushions of counterfeit arras, a long cushion and two short ones of blue velvet, also two carpets. Arras is tapestry woven with figures and scenes, and sarsenet is a very fine and soft silk. For son-in-law George, Earl of Shrewsbury, and daughter Anne, his wife, there were some ecclesiastical vestments and several other things: a primer (or book of hours) which Katharine's sister Alice, Lady Fitzhugh, had in her care; two cushions of counterfeit arras and three cushions of blue velvet; coverings of purple velvet for cushions, and two carpets.

After her daughters Lady Hastings remembered her sons. The eldest, Edward, had had a rich marriage arranged for him by his father. The bride was Mary Hungerford, heiress to her great-grandmother's barony of Botreaux and her grandfather's baronies of Hungerford and Moleyns. The Hungerfords had been prominent Lancastrian supporters, and Mary's grandfather, Robert, had been taken prisoner and beheaded at the battle of Hexham in 1464. Her father, Thomas, had been hanged as a traitor in 1469. Mary was then about two years old, and by 1472 William Hastings had secured her wardship and the right to arrange her marriage. She was married to Edward Hastings in 1479, when she was about twelve and he was a year or two older. In 1482 Edward was summoned to parliament as a lord in right of his wife's barony of Hungerford. The following is a list of his mother's bequests to Edward, Lord Hastings. A set of vestments; a precious buckle or brooch; an image of the Virgin Mary; a gold salt-cellar; a fair primer, which had been given to Katharine, Lady Hastings, by Queen Elizabeth, who could be either Elizabeth

Woodville or her daughter Elizabeth of York, the wife of Henry VII of England; two coverings of counterfeit arras for cushions; two cushions of counterfeit arras, with William, Lord Hastings', arms; two pairs of curtains of green tartarin, which was a rich stuff, apparently of silk, imported from the east; two short cushions of tawny velvet; one long and one short cushion of tawny velvet; some hangings which were used in the church at Ashby-de-la-Zouch and others from the hall and chapel at Ashby castle; 'all such pieces of hangings as I have of blue and better blue, with my lord's arms, with banners and cupboard clothes of the same sort'; three bare hides for carriage and two for cloth sacks: a bare hide being presumably a hide with the hair removed or one undressed; the third part of the hay at Kirby Muxloe and all the timber which Lady Hastings had there; 'all the bedding that he hath of mine, which late was at London, reserved only two feather beds and a couch, that I will Richard my son have'; two carpets. Lady Hastings' other chief beneficiaries were her sons Richard and William, who seem to have been keeping house together; her youngest son George got very little. Finally there were some small legacies, including a distribution of dresses amongst Lady Hastings' female servants, 'and one old gown to Mother Ceall, of Leicester'.

The Hastings Hours

Two primers are mentioned in Lady Hastings' will, 'my primer which is now in the keeping of my Lady Fitzhugh' and 'a fair primer which I had by the gesture of Queen Elizabeth'. The word primer was used in the fourteenth and fifteenth centuries for the book of services and prayers now usually described as a book of hours; and it will be recalled that two books of hours survive which are connected with William, Lord Hastings. They are the manuscript which is the subject of this edition and the other in Madrid. Neither can so far be safely identified with either of the books in Lady Hastings' will.

Books of hours were very popular in the later Middle Ages and the Renaissance, and they range from such sumptuous volumes as the famous manuscript which is known as the *Très Riches Heures* of the Duke of Berry, made towards the beginning of the fifteenth century for the French royal prince of that name, to quite modest books devoid of decoration. Possession of a book of hours was symbolic as much as devotional: to have one was not necessary for salvation, but one was clearly part of the furniture of anybody of any standing in this world who hoped for a reasonable place in the next.

The contents of a book of hours represented a simplification of the full round of the church's daily services of praise and prayer which do not include the central service: the mass, or eucharist. In principle the church addressed its maker eight times a day; the services for these times were known as hours, or, more fully, canonical hours, because, a canon being a rule or discipline, they were appropriated to certain of the twenty-four hours. The names of the different canonical hours are matins, lauds, prime, terce, sext, none, vespers, and compline. Together they make up what is known as the divine office. Other services for daily use developed which resembled, but were less elaborate than, the divine office. Chief of these was the office of the Blessed Virgin Mary, which emphasized Mary's special place in Christianity, her *rôle* as mediatrix of all graces. The hours of the Virgin were understandably popular and are the main and indispensable component of a book of hours, that which gives it its name. Another usual ingredient is the office of the dead, by which the faithful pray for the departed who have not yet attained heaven. This office comprises only vespers, matins, and lauds.

The basis of the divine and similar offices is scriptural, psalms and passages from the other parts of the Bible. To this was added non-scriptural material, in particular hymns and prayers. Down to the later sixteenth century there was not a little local variation in the services of the western church. Despite, perhaps because of, the Pope of Rome's claim to supremacy in the church, whilst the liturgical practices and usages – the 'use' – of Rome obtained widespread adherence, the 'use' of other centres, or of religious orders, was often preferred. In the Hastings Houses the use of the office of the Virgin and the office of the dead is that of Sarum, the ecclesiastical name for Salisbury, in Wiltshire. The customs of Salisbury cathedral largely provided the norm for services in the church in England from the thirteenth century to the reformation.

This may seem surprising, since the ecclesiastical capital of England was Canterbury. The reason is probably a peculiarity of the pre-reformation church in England and Wales, which was that of its twenty-one cathedrals nine, including Canterbury, were staffed by Benedictine monks and were in fact monasteries. Monastic liturgical usage is too far removed from that of non-monastic churches for these to take it as their model. Salisbury was the leading non-monastic cathedral in England.

The liturgical 'use' of a book of hours or other service book – such as a missal, which contains the texts for mass, or a breviary, which contains the divine office – is far from determining where, or for where, or for whom, the book was made; but it does supply useful evidence for localization. More direct evidence often comes from the interest in various saints which is shown in a book.

Every day the church recalls numerous events and figures in her history, but only a few of these merit formal commemoration. Some of these commemorations, like Christmas or Easter or the feast of Sts Peter and Paul, are general, others are only local observances. As a guide to commemorations, and dating – for to the middle ages the church year was if anything more important than the civil year – calendars appear in liturgical books. They necessarily exclude mention of days which are movable, such as Easter and those dependent on it, like Ascension day and Whit Sunday, although Easter at least may be entered on the traditional, but arbitrary, date of 27 March. Further, the church does not observe its feast days and fast days with equal importance, and again, whilst the degree of attention given to some days – in particular the high days, like again Christmas or Easter or the feast of Sts Peter and Paul – is general, special attention is only given to others locally. The grading of an entry in a caldendar may be shown by some liturgical note attached to it or by the manner of writing, especially by the use of different coloured inks, with black naturally being normally used for ordinary days and red frequently for more important ones. Sometimes several colours are employed, in a scale. The appearance in a calendar in a service book of local saints' days highly graded is most indicative for finding the provenance of the book.

The Hastings Hours begins with a calendar (ff. 1–12b), which has entries in red and black. These allow some narrowing of designation within the domain of the Sarum rite. The most informative entries in red are those of the feast of St Hugh, bishop of Lincoln 1186–1200, with an octave, on 17 November, and of his Translation on 6 October. An octave is the celebration of a feast for a full week, that is, eight days, including the original day of the feast and the corresponding day a week later. Only the very highest feasts, like Christmas and Easter, always have octaves, and the provision of a local feast like that of Hugh of Lincoln with one elevates it to the first rank. Translation is the solemn removal of a saint's body or relics to a more worthy place. The calendar in the Hastings Hours was clearly intended for use in the diocese of Lincoln, which, in pre-reformation England, was of vast extent, touching in the north the river Humber and in the south the Thames. Within it were the Hastings family lands and seats in Leicestershire.

In general the calendar in the Hastings Hours is a mixture of English, north French, and Flemish interests. There was a type of calendar which can be described as Sarum, but the Hastings calendar is not one such. The English saints in it, besides Hugh of Lincoln, are Edmund, King of East Anglia, who was martyred in 869 (20 November, in red); Chad, the seventh-century bishop of Lichfield (2 March); Edward, King of England, who was martyred in 979 (18 March); Alphege, archbishop of Canterbury, who was martyred in 1012 (19 April); John of Beverley, the eighth-century bishop of York (7 May); Dunstan, the famous archbishop of Canterbury 960–988 (19 May); Augustine, the first archbishop of Canterbury (26 May); Boniface, the apostle of Germany (5 June); the Translation of Swithun, the ninth-century bishop of Winchester (15 July); Oswald, King of Northumbria, who was martyred in 642 (5 August); Paulinus, the first bishop of York (10 October); Etheldreda, the foundress of the abbey of Ely (17 October); Frideswide, the patron saint of Oxford (19 October); Willibrord, the apostle of the Netherlands (7 November); Edmund Rich, archbishop of Canterbury 1233–40 (16 November).

At the end of the middle ages people attached excessive importance to the saints, those departed Christians who, being thought to have reached heaven and to enjoy sight of God, were peculiarly placed to intercede with him for the faithful on earth. They were the subject of many devotions, one of the oldest of which is the litany of the saints: a series of petitions, the majority of which implore a saint or saints for their prayers. A litany of the saints is a usual ingredient in a book of hours, and the invocations often include ones to saints of local or personal importance, local to the place where or for which a book was produced, or personal to the man or woman for whom it was produced. The Hastings Hours has a litany (ff.172–179b), which invokes twenty martyrs, twenty-four confessors, that is, male saints who witnessed to the faith without being put to death for it, and twenty-seven virgins. None of them appears to have local or personal significance. Nor do the saints to whom a series of prayers are addressed at lauds of the Virgin Mary. Such commemorations or memorials of saints, as they were called, are frequently found at lauds and also vespers in the office of the Virgin.

More interesting is a series of twenty-two memorials of saints (ff.38–72) which occur towards the beginning of the Hastings Hours. Each of these memorials was originally illustrated with a miniature, five of which are now missing. In any arrangement of saints, in a litany or a series of prayers, an order of precedence was followed, and the placing of a saint higher than might be expected denoted a local or personal patron. Further, there was a rule that only the Virgin Mary and otherworldly saints, by which are meant angels, should normally rank higher than John the Baptist, for Christ had said, 'Among them born of women there hath not risen a greater than John the Baptist.'

The twenty-two memorials of saints towards the beginning of the Hastings Hours start with prayers to St Paul, St Leonard, St David of Wales, St Jerome, and the Three Kings, or Magi. Then come St John the Baptist, St Adrian, St George, St Christopher, St Anthony the Great, Sts Fabian and Sebastian, St Erasmus, St Thomas Becket, St Nicholas, the Virgin Mary, St Anne, St Margaret, St Elizabeth of Hungary, St Sitha, St Katharine of Alexandria, and St Barbara.

The memorials are preceded by other devotions and prayers, which are also illustrated with miniatures (ff.18b–37b). There were four of these miniatures, but the first and last are missing. The second and third show the Mass of St Gregory (f.18b) and the

Holy Trinity (f.20b); the texts that were associated with them suggest that the first and fourth miniatures were of St John the Evangelist and the Virgin Mary. Mary's portrait would have faced a prayer to her, and the Evangelist's picture would have been connected with another frequent item in books of hours, namely, short extracts from the gospels of John, Luke, Matthew, and Mark. The passage from John tells of the incarnation of the word of God, that from Luke is the story of the annunciation to Mary, the reading from Matthew is about the adoration of the newborn Christ by the Magi, and from Mark is taken the account of Christ's mission of the apostles into the world and his ascension. In the Hastings Hours the gospel extracts follow immediately after the calendar (ff.13–17b).

It will be noticed that there is an interest in the legend of the Mass of St Gregory. This tale of a demonstration of the real presence of Christ in the sacrament of the altar was dear to fifteenth- and sixteenth-century Christians in western Europe, especially in Germany and Flanders, but it does seem to have been given special prominence in the Hastings Hours. It is worth recalling that in 1472 William, Lord Hastings, and his brother Ralph founded a confraternity in honour of the Holy Cross, called 'the Holy Rood in the Wall', in the church of St Gregory, Northampton. The purpose of the confraternity was to support chaplains to celebrate divine service for the good estate of the king, and his consort, Elizabeth, Queen of England, and their descendants, and the founders and other brethren and sisters of the confraternity, and for their souls after death, and the souls of the king's father Richard, late Duke of York, and the king's progenitors.

There is no available reason why the Three Kings should be commemorated in the Hastings Hours before John the Baptist, but Paul, Leonard, David, and Jerome are thrown into further relief by the manner of execution of their miniatures and texts.

All the miniatures in the Hastings Hours are insertions into the textual scheme of the book, as was usual in books of hours originating in the Low Countries at the time. Examination of the way in which the Hastings Hours is bound reveals that it is made up of five entities and one special feature. The entities are (i) the calendar, ff.1–12b; (ii) the gospel extracts, the devotions, and the hours of the Virgin, ff.13–149b; (iii) the penitential psalms, the gradual psalms, and the litany, ff.151–183b; (iv) the office of the dead, the commendation of souls, and the psalms of the passion, ff.185–264b; (v) the Fifteen Prayers and the Psalter of St Jerome, ff.276–297b. There are twenty-eight miniatures in the Hastings Hours now, and seven more have been lost. With the exception of the pictures of Paul, Leonard, David of Wales, and Jerome, all the miniatures are, or were, on the verso of single folios, the recto of which is blank. Each is surrounded by an ornamental border, but does not share its page with any writing. It has been put into the manuscript to face the beginning of a text which it illustrates and the facing text-page is itself adorned with an ornamental or, in five instances, historiated border. Seven text-pages with ornamental borders survive which once were complemented by miniatures.

Paul (f.38), Leonard (f.39), David (f.40), and Jerome (f.41) are also each on single folios, but on the recto. They have ornamental borders around them, but their pages also contain some lines of text, which is continued on the verso. The commemorations and representations of Paul, Leonard, David, and Jerome are clearly a special feature in the Hastings Hours, presumably there at the express wish of the person for whom the book was made.

No explanation has been found for an interest by William, Lord Hastings, in Paul and Jerome, and it is rare to find St Paul enjoying attention by himself and not in conjunction with St Peter. Leonard, it will be recalled, was the name of William Hastings' father. The portrayal of St David of Wales is the only one known in an illuminated manuscript. He is shown not as a bishop, but as a prince, in accordance with the story of his royal birth. The life and legend of St David are further discussed in the commentary to the reproduction of the miniature of him. This miniature did, however, originally intend to depict a bishop. It is not difficult to decipher in it a bishop's mitre where now is a royal coronet and a bishop's crozier where now is a royal sceptre. Why the emphasis on Wales and a prince of Wales? Hastings was chamberlain of north Wales and constable of Harlech castle, and Edward IV always took a close interest in Wales, but something more is needed to explain the miniature in the Hastings Hours. Presumably it witnesses to a devotion by William, Lord Hastings, to the future of the Yorkist kings in the person of Edward IV's heir apparent, Edward, Prince of Wales and afterwards, but briefly, King Edward V.

On four pages in the Hastings Hours are the arms of Hastings (ff.13, 74, 151, 184b). In all cases they are additions to the manuscript. On f.13, in the right-hand border, is the Hastings shield, surrounded by the Garter and surmounted by a helmet and mantling and the Hastings crest. On ff.74 and 151 just the shield, surrounded by the Garter, is in the right-hand border. On f.184b the arms have been incorporated into a miniature. The scene is a funeral. Two rows of black robed mourners kneel and sit on either side of a coffin, draped with a pall, over which is a hearse with candles. Surpliced clerics are in stalls on either side. On the pall is a shield and there are two more on the hearse. Attached to a chandelier above is a black hanging with a row of shields on it. All the shields once contained the royal arms of England. Over them have been painted the arms of Hastings. Supported by the chandelier are four banners. One of them formerly bore the royal arms of England, which are now overpainted with the Hastings arms, the other three retain their original designs. Again, these are heraldic, but the coats have not been identified. The blasons are (i) gules, two bars over three estoiles or; (ii) bendy sinister, or and sable, with an indistinct chief; (iii) or, a chevron between three martlets sable.

The arms of England are also part of the original decoration of another page in the Hastings Hours. On f.126 the text of the beginning of the hour of none of the Virgin is surrounded by a border in which a royal barge is rowed on a river. In the bow stand two men blowing long trumpets to which are attached banners with the royal arms of England. A long streamer in red and blue, the royal colours of England, with on it the first word of the motto of the order of the Garter, hangs from a tall flagstaff in the prow. The presence of the English arms on this page, and also at one time on that with the miniature of a funeral, led Sir George Warner, when cataloguing the Hastings Hours in 1920 for C.W. Dyson Perrins, who then owned it, to suggest that the manuscript might originally have belonged to Henry VII, king of England 1485 to 1509, or his son Henry VIII, who was king from 1509 to 1547. The Hastings arms Warner connected not with William, Lord Hastings, but with his great-grandson Edward, who was made a baron in 1558. Warner reasoned that Edward Hastings became a knight of the Garter in 1555 and that he must have obtained the manuscript between then and his elevation to the peerage because there is no coronet together with the Hastings arms. This argument presumably also excluded the other members of the Hastings family who received the garter, who were Edward's elder brother Francis, Francis' son Henry, and the ancestor of them all, William, Edward IV's friend. It has already been remarked that William was created a baron in 1461 and a knight of the Garter in 1462. Francis Hastings succeeded as Earl of Huntingdon in 1545 and was made a knight of the Garter in 1549. He died in 1560 and Henry Hastings became Earl of Huntingdon, receiving the garter in 1570.

Warner is too exacting. Heraldic representations were not precise enough for anything to be deduced from the absence of a coronet above the shield of Hastings arms. The circumstantial evidence is that the person denoted is William, Lord Hastings. The strongest piece of this evidence is the prominence given in the book of hours to a commemoration and representation of Leonard, the name-saint of William's father. Then there is the probable interest in Pope St Gregory the Great, in whose church, at Northampton, William and his brother Ralph had founded a confraternity. One of the historiated borders may also be considered. On f.43 the beginning of the memorial of the Three Kings is surrounded by a scene of money being thrown to people in a distribution of largesse. William, Lord Hastings, as master of the mint was the moneyer of England. It is true that the subjects in the ornamentation of an illuminated manuscript of the period of the Hastings Hours were far from being unique or original, and its scene of largesse can be paralleled in another book of hours of Flemish origin, now in the Bibliothèque Royale, Brussels (MS. IV. 280, f.205). This manuscript is of the 'use' of Bruges and datable shortly after 1500. However, because a subject was available does not mean that it could not be selected deliberately. The coincidence seems too great of distribution of money and a coat of arms which could be that of a master of the mint.

Finally, there is a point of comparison with the Hastings Hours in Madrid. It is not certain that this manuscript either was owned by William, Lord Hastings. Its connexion with him depends primarily on the occurrence on one of the pages at the beginning of the book (f.iv) of a shield with the Hastings arms, surrounded by the Garter, and surmounted by a helmet and mantling and the Hastings crest. The argument from heraldry is thus the same as for the Hastings Hours in London. The Madrid manuscript contains a calendar (ff.2–13b) which is not markedly close to that in the London manuscript. Then it has devotions, memorials of the saints, and gospel extracts (ff.14–71). The main series of memorials of the saints numbers fifteen, and with the omission of a memorial of St Thomas Becket, is the same as the series from John the Baptist to Barbara in the London manuscript. The series is not standard and its presence in two manuscripts which have been related by being assigned to the same ownership must be intentional.

The suggestion of a royal patron for the Hastings Hours in London (which for the present publication it is convenient to call the Hastings Hours *tout court*) is tempting, but does not withstand scrutiny. The royal barge on f.126 need not be interpreted as more than implying close connexion with the court. It is the funeral miniature on f.184b which is more important. The composition is stock, to be found in other illuminated manuscripts of the same origin and time as the Hastings Hours, namely, the Ghent-Bruges workshops of the late fifteenth and the early sixteenth century. Here are six examples.

1. The Book of Hours and Benedictional made *circa* 1485 probably for Philip II Conrault, abbot of the Benedictine abbey of Mont Blandin, Ghent (Oxford, Bodleian Library, MS. Douce 223), f.106b.

2. The Book of Hours in Vienna made *circa* 1485 for Philip of Cleves, Lord of Ravenstein, a prominent Flemish statesman (Vienna, Österreichische Nationalbibliothek, Cod. ser. nov. 13239), f.151b.

3. The Hours of Isabella the Catholic, Queen of Castile 1474 to 1504, made *circa* 1492 (Cleveland, Museum of Art, 63. 256), f.219b.

4. The Book of Hours made *circa* 1503 for James IV, King of Scotland 1488 to 1513 (Vienna, Österreichische Nationalbibliothek, Cod. 1897), f.141.

5. The Grimani Breviary, executed *circa* 1515 and acquired by

Cardinal Domenico Grimani, patriarch of Aquileia, in 1520 (Venice, Biblioteca Marciana, MS. Lat. I, 99), f.45.
6. The Hortulus Animae (in English, 'Garden of the Soul'), a devotional anthology copied from an edition printed at Strasbourg in 1510 and executed *circa* 1515 (Vienna, Österreichische Nationalbibliothek, Cod. 2706), f.454b.

In the funeral miniatures in the Grimani Breviary and the *Hortulus Animae* shields are provided for armorial bearings, but they have been left blank. In the Conrault Hours, the Cleves Hours, the Isabella Hours, and the James IV Hours there are shields and banners which have armorial devices. Those in the Conrault, Cleves, and Isabella Hours have not been identified. They could be merely decorative, as could the unidentified arms on the banners in the funeral miniature in the Hastings Hours. In the funeral in the James IV Hours there are the royal arms of Scotland.

If the English royal arms in the funeral in the Hastings Hours, together with its scene of the royal barge, mean that the manuscript was originally for an English royal personage, this seems to be belied by other contents of the book. Why should English royalty want a Lincoln diocese calendar? Admittedly, the Woodvilles came from Grafton in Northamptonshire, and Queen Elizabeth Woodville's first husband was a Leicestershire knight. Northamptonshire, like Leicestershire, was in the diocese of Lincoln. This raises the question of the primer given to Katharine, Lady Hastings, by a Queen Elizabeth. Elizabeth Woodville would very likely have been interested in having a representation of a Prince of Wales in a book of hours made for her, and in having an episcopal likeness of St David of Wales altered into a royal semblance. There is no obvious reason why she should have a special devotion to St Leonard, unless she regarded the sanctuary at Westminster, to which she retired during Edward IV's eclipse in 1470 to 1471 and where she gave birth to her eldest son, as a prison from which she was delivered at the intercession of the saint. She could also have attributed the safe birth of the child as due to Leonard. St Leonard's patronage of women in labour and people in prison is discussed in the commentary on the reproduction of his miniature. Edward V was indeed born shortly before St Leonard's feast day of 6 November, on one of the days between 1 and 4 November.

However, any interest by Queen Elizabeth Woodville in St Leonard is conjecture, although if the idea of associating the Hastings Hours with her is being pursued the presence of the highly graded commemoration of St Paul in the manuscript could be regarded as due to the fact that the queen's maternal grandfather was Count of St Pol in Luxembourg. Albeit, his name was Pierre, which makes even more strange the absence of a memorial and representation of St Peter to complement those of St Paul. There is no trace of such having been lost.

The argumentation is becoming fanciful, and it seems wiser to attempt a return to reality by remembering the similarity between the series of memorials of the saints towards the beginning of the two Hastings Hours, in London and Madrid. There is no suspicion of a royal commission about the Madrid book. All in all, the most likely hypothesis is that both the Madrid and London Hastings Hours were made to the order of William, Lord Hastings, and that the arms of England were set in the funeral miniature in the London book as suitable for a manuscript destined for the English market. Hastings decided to make the allusion more personal. It seems to have been Otto Pächt, to whom the history of art owes so much, who, with the assistance of John Armstrong, that expert historian of fifteenth-century England and Burgundy, first assigned the British Library's manuscript to William, Lord Hastings.

The Hastings Master

For the two books of hours Hastings turned to the leading manufacturers of fine hand-made books at the time, the scribes and illuminators of Flanders. English manuscript illumination had been in utter decline since the middle of the fifteenth century. The same period saw the rise of Flemish manuscript illumination to an excellence second to none. The climate which favoured this was that of the northern Renaissance, which received its patronage from the Dukes of Burgundy and their court and was financed, as were the Dukes of Burgundy, by the commerce of

Flanders, with its two capitals of Ghent and Bruges. Bruges was the old capital of Flanders, but after 1180 Ghent had taken the lead, although Bruges equalled it in wealth and power until access to the sea was stopped by the silting up of the estuary of the river Zwijn, which was complete by 1490.

In the period to which the Hastings Hours may be attributed on grounds of style, namely, *circa* 1480, one of the richest citizens of Bruges was the painter Hans Memlinc, who had arrived there *circa* 1465 and was to die there in 1494. Hastings was surely not unacquainted with Memlinc's work, since the Donne Triptych of the Virgin and Child with Sts Katharine, Barbara, John the Baptist and John the Evangelist, now in the National Gallery, London, was painted by Memlinc for Hastings' sister and brother-in-law, Sir John and Lady Donne. Memlinc's successor as the leading Bruges artist was Gerard David, who was active there in 1484 and died there in 1523. In the meantime Ghent had seen the troubled and talented Hugo van der Goes. He was admitted a master painter at Ghent in 1467. In 1475 he entered the religious life, at the house of Augustinian canons called the Roode Clooster, near Brussels. In 1482 he died there, having been mad for about a year.

For the graphic arts the Renaissance meant the emergence of the panel painting as the chief vehicle of expression. Previously this had been the miniature in a manuscript. Manuscript illumination was now challenged, and threatened. Its story in the fifteenth and sixteenth centuries is the story of how it responded. Only the Flemish illuminators succeeded in developing a Renaissance style of book painting and illustration which was other than a dependant of panel painting. This they achieved in the works of what Count Paul Durrieu in 1891 named the Ghent-Bruges school. Its period is from about the time of the death of Duke Charles 'the Bold' of Burgundy in 1477 to *circa* 1530. In his monumental *La miniature flamande au temps de la Cour de Bourgogne*, published in 1921, Durrieu characterized the school in terms which still retain their validity. They may be summarized in the statement that, whereas, in the time of Philip 'the Good' and Charles 'the Bold', Flemish illumination had evoked the art of Roger van der Weyden and Dieric Bouts, subsequently it reflected that of Memlinc, Gerard David, and Quinten Massys.

In 1948 Otto Pächt made a vital contribution to the study of the origins of the school with his *The Master of Mary of Burgundy*. Pächt went so far as to claim that the artist about whom he was writing 'was undoubtedly the founder of the famous Ghent-Bruges school of miniaturists' and to say that practically the whole of the school stood on the Master's shoulders. The Master of Mary of Burgundy was an anonymous artist who derived his name from being supposed to have illuminated two books of hours between 1477 and 1482 for Mary, only child of Charles 'the Bold' of Burgundy by his second wife, Isabella of Bourbon, and her husband Maximilian of Austria. Mary was Duchess of Burgundy from 1477 till she was killed in a riding accident in 1482. Maximilian was to be the ruler of Germany from 1493 till his death in 1519. The two books of hours are Vienna, Österreichische Nationalbibliothek, Cod. 1857, and Berlin, Kupferstich-kabinett, MS. 78 B. 12.

Recently the identity of the Master of Mary of Burgundy has been questioned, in particular by G.I. Lieftinck in *Boekverluchters uit de Omgeving van Maria van Bourgondië*, 1969. The Master of Mary of Burgundy is receding as the inventor of the Ghent-Bruges school of illumination. After Lieftinck interest has been shifting towards another anonymous artist who is seen as the first exponent of the Ghent-Bruges style and has been baptized with the unwieldy name of the Master of the Older Prayerbook of Maximilian I. Maximilian I is the widower of Mary of Burgundy, who became the Roman Emperor Maximilian I, Roman Emperor being the title of the ruler of Germany. A necessary preliminary to becoming emperor was to be chosen 'King of the Romans' by the leading princes of Germany. This happened to Maximilian in 1486. In connexion with the event he commissioned from the Flemish workshops a manuscript collection of prayers which contains illumination by the artist who is named after it, the Master of the First, or Older, Prayerbook of Maximilian I. (The Second, or Younger, Prayerbook of Maximilian I is a book of hours which the emperor ordered to be printed in 1508. It was produced at Augsburg in 1514.)

Attempts are being made to identify the Maximilian Master as Alexander Bening, a Flemish illuminator whose existence is documented, but no works by whom have ever been established with certainty. Alexander Bening was admitted to the guild of painters and sculptors at Ghent in 1469, among his sponsors being Hugo van der Goes. In 1480 Alexander married Katharine van der Goes, who was either Hugo's sister or his niece. Alexander was admitted to the guild of illuminators and booksellers at Bruges in 1486. He died at Ghent in 1519.

Alexander's son Simon was the greatest master of the Ghent-Bruges school, and appears to have been a panel painter as well as a miniaturist. Simon had a daughter, Lievine, who also practised the two disciplines. She came to England at the request of Henry VIII and was in favour with his two daughters Mary I (reigned 1553–58) and Elizabeth I (1558–1603).

One masterpiece of Flemish illumination which has never been properly evaluated is the Hastings Hours. Assuming it was completed before the sudden death of William, Lord Hastings, in 1483, it ranks as the earliest known monument of the Ghent-Bruges school. Previously this had been thought to be Maximilian's manuscript of 1486, but in any case the illumination in the Hastings Hours considerably outranks that in the Prayerbook. A deal of detailed study of Flemish manuscript illumination in the last quarter of the fifteenth century is needed, and a special study of the Hastings Hours, before a clear picture emerges of what was really happening. Such an examination is outside the scope of the present publication, but readers who would like to know how thinking is developing are recommended to consult 'The Master of Mary of Burgundy and his Colleagues: The State of Research and Questions of Method' by Anne H. van Buren in *Zeitschrift für Kunstgeschichte*, Band 38, 1975, pp. 286–309 and 'A Book of Hours of Queen Isabel la Católica' by Patrick M. de Winter in *The Bulletin of the Cleveland Museum of Art*, lxvii, 1981, pp. 342–427. They will also find much of value in the description by Joachim M. Plotzek in Anton von Euw and Joachim M. Plotzek, *Die Handschriften der Sammlung Ludwig*, 2, 1982, pp. 256–85, of a book of hours executed *circa* 1515, which belonged probably to Margaret of Austria, the daughter of Mary of Burgundy and Maximilian I. The present essay will attempt only some appreciation of the excellent work of art which is the Hastings Hours.

A book such as this was a thoroughly commercial product, in

which quite a number of people would share. There would be at least three persons involved: one to do the writing, one to do the initials and borders, and one to do the miniatures. The miniaturist at least would probably have assistants, and it is common to find in a Renaissance book of hours miniatures by more than one master painter and his assistants. The script of the Hastings Hours appears to be by the same man as that in the Madrid Hastings Hours, the Hours of Mary of Burgundy in Berlin, the Hours of Philip of Cleves in Vienna, and another book of hours of the same date, also made for Philip of Cleves, which is now MS. IV. 40 in the Bibliothèque Royale, Brussels. It is a clear, well-formed hand of the type usual in Flemish books of the period. The Hastings Hours has no decoration in the margins of the majority of its pages, and there is none of the calendar decoration which is such a feature of many books of hours. The ornamentation is concentrated on the beginning of sections or items, such as the series of memorials of the saints on ff.38–72, the hours of the Virgin, and the office of the dead. The scheme was for a page of text to be surrounded by a border and faced by a miniature likewise surrounded. An addition to this scheme is the four special miniatures of Sts Paul, Leonard, David, and Jerome (ff.38, 39, 40, 41). In so far as pictorial decoration of the Hastings Hours has a theme it is that of the birth of Christ, which is pursued by the illustrations to the hours of the Virgin. This is usual in books of hours of the date and provenance of the Hastings Hours.

The majority of the borders in the manuscript are composed of a coloured ground bearing naturalistic flowers and foliage, with which are associated butterflies, dragonflies, flies, snails, and birds. The flowers and foliage and the other motifs are not meant to be so much on the coloured ground as in front of it, and the illusion of this is created by providing them with shadows. This trick also ensures that there is an illusion of a strong light shining on the illuminated pages, from the direction of the top left. A complex illusion of recession results. The borders have frames and the inner frames, around a miniature or a page of text, also cast shadows. Thus, the ground in the borders appears as a kind of trough in which decorative motifs are suspended. The pages of text have no recession themselves, but because the inner frame of a border has its shadow the area of text also seems to be floating. In fact, the illusion attempted is not one of a page with a border, but of a coloured background in front of which are a panel bearing texts and decorative motifs. The illusion on a miniature page is different, since the miniatures have depth. The effect here of having a recessed ground for the borders is to increase the depth in the miniatures, so that there are two kinds of space in the miniature pages, a finite one in the borders and an infinite one in the pictures. The techniques of depth used in the illumination of the Hastings Hours should not be regarded as the technique of a particular artist, but as a technique of Flemish illuminators. The ornamental borders in the manuscript are unlikely to be by the same hand as the miniatures, and it looks as if the majority of the borders around the miniatures are by a different hand from that which was responsible for the ornamental borders around pages of text. The facing ornamental borders are closely related in style, but the only ones which might have been designed with reference to each other seem to be on ff.55b and 56 (representation and memorial of St Thomas Becket) and ff.73b and 74 (miniature of the Annunciation and beginning of matins of the Virgin). Even in these cases the painting of each pair of borders seems to be the work of two hands, one for the verso page and the other for the recto.

All the miniatures in the Hastings Hours appear to be by one artist, which does not exclude their being the work of more than one person. The point is that even if they are due to one master and one or more assistants, they are due to one artistic personality. It is foolish to expect autograph works of art in the period of the Hastings Hours, and those who do should read Max Friedländer's chapter on 'Workshop Production' in his book *On Art and Connoisseurship*. When examining miniatures in mediaeval and Renaissance manuscripts it is important to determine not how many hands held the brushes that painted them, but how many minds inspired hand and brush. It is perfectly legitimate to speak of the miniaturist of the Hastings Hours and to call him the Master of the same. He is probably the same artist as the one who goes under the name of the Master of the Older Prayerbook of Maximilian I, but this name becomes even more unsatisfactory when it is realized that the miniatures in Maximilian's manuscript are of secondary quality, not attributable to the Master in the way that the miniatures in the Hastings Hours are, and should not be used as a touchstone for the Master's style. This really emerges, and so for the first time does the Ghent-Bruges style, in the Hastings Hours.

The best miniatures of the Ghent-Bruges school do not have to be regarded as miniature in a pejorative sense: this even when their compositions are obviously derived from panel painting. The source for the Nativity in the Hastings Hours (f.106b) was the altarpiece of the Nativity which Hugo van der Goes painted for Tommaso Portinari, the agent in Ghent of the Medici family, and sent to Florence in 1475–76. It is now in the Uffizi Gallery, Florence. The format in which a picture was contained was not something about which mediaeval illuminators had had to worry, for their art was abstract. It became a concern at the Renaissance when art became naturalistic and panel paintings became the norm. The dilemma now for any painter was: was he to paint what he saw or what he felt about what he saw? The danger inherent in representational painting is the inclusion of too much detail. This, with the relatively small scale available to illuminators, was what destroyed miniatures in books.

The Master of Mary of Burgundy seems to have dealt with the problem by adopting an illusionistic style and contenting himself with being a painter in miniature. In his most successful work, a book of hours which belonged to Engelbert, count of Nassau, governor of the Low Countries from 1501 till his death in 1504, now MS. Douce 219–20 in the Bodleian Library, Oxford, his compositions give the appearance of diminishing always more and more.

The Master of the Hastings Hours has a stronger and sharper style. The perspective is excellent, whether it is a case of an outdoor scene receding into a far distance of hills and trees and buildings, as with St Sitha on f.67, or an indoor scene in a church carefully bounded by an ambulatory and a rich hanging behind the central figure as with St Nicholas on f.57b. The balance in the pictures is just right. In French illumination of the period the artist Jean Colombe was crowding miniatures with people and events in a way which betrays an obsession with space. The figures in the Hastings Hours move through landscape and buildings which are familiar in Flemish painting from the time of the Master of Flémalle and Jan van Eyck, but the Flemish *paysage* has never been transferred to the pages of a book so successfully before the Hastings Hours. Particularly good is the Hastings Master's depiction of water, which appears limpid with clear reflections. A very fine example of the treatment of water by the Hastings Master is in the frontispiece to a Chronicle of the Princes of Cleves, Cod. gall. 19 in the Bayerische Staatsbibliothek, Munich, which was probably written and illuminated for Philip of Cleves in the early 1480s. Here the knight of the swan, the founder of the house of Cleves, sails in his boat, guided by the swan. The Master of the Hastings Hours works well with grey tones, especially for stone interiors, as in the churchly settings for St Leonard on f.39, St David on f.40, or St Nicholas on f.57b. Whereas the figures in many contemporary Flemish miniatures are doll-like, those in the Hastings Hours are very real, and sentimentality appears only once, in the picture of the Virgin and Child on f.59b.

Nothing is known surely of the history of the Hastings Hours before 1910, when it was purchased by C.W. Dyson Perrins from the booksellers Bernard Quaritch for the high price for then of £2200. Quaritch have not been able to trace whence they acquired the manuscript. Charles William Dyson Perrins was born on 25 May 1864, his father being one of the original partners in the firm of Lea & Perrins, the propagators of the celebrated Worcester sauce. It was the money from Worcester sauce which was to enable C.W. Dyson Perrins to become a great collector and benefactor. To him the Worcester Royal Grammar School owes a hall and a science laboratory, Malvern the Rose Bank house and gardens and a hospital, and Oxford University a science laboratory. During the years 1900 to 1920 Dyson Perrins was particularly active as a book collector. In 1946 he decided to sell his printed books, so as to benefit the Royal Worcester Porcelain Factory, in which he had always been interested. The Factory was the recipient of his fine collection of Worcester china.

When he died on 29 January 1958 Dyson Perrins left behind a collection of one hundred and sixty-one illuminated manuscripts, ranging in date over eleven hundred years, from the ninth to the twentieth centuries. Whilst most were of European provenance, there was also Armenian and Persian and Indian material. Two of the greatest treasures were bequeathed to the British Museum: the Gorleston Psalter, written and illuminated in England in the fourteenth century, and the *Khamsah* of Niẓāmī, written and illuminated for the Mogul emperor Akbar in AD 1595. Dyson Perrins' executors allowed the British Museum to acquire eight more manuscripts privately, at favourable terms. Virtually all the rest of the collection was dispersed at public auction in 1958 to 1960, but two items remained, kept by Dyson Perrins' widow. They were a manual of prayers, executed in Italy, perhaps at Naples, in the sixteenth century, which Dyson Perrins had given to his wife on 25 May 1930, and the Hastings Hours. When Mrs Perrins died, on 28 December 1968, she was found to have bequeathed her two manuscripts to the British Museum.

Commentaries on the Plates

18b Devout Prayer to Jesus Christ: the Mass of St Gregory

The first prayer in the Hastings Hours is addressed to the Christ, who, on the cross, prayed for forgiveness for his enemies because 'they know not what they do'. Facing is a miniature of the Mass of St Gregory, a subject popular in the fifteenth and sixteenth centuries, especially in Germany and Flanders. The legend illustrated dates from the late middle ages and is not part of the original cycle of stories surrounding Pope Gregory I (reigned 590–604). It tells how, in order that those serving the pope at mass might be strengthened in faith in the real presence of Christ in the sacrament, the Man of Sorrows appeared at the pope's mass. Gregory kneels at the altar with a cardinal kneeling to either side. Above the altar is the tomb of Christ, with Christ standing in it, wounded and crowned with thorns, and behind him is the cross. On his left is the column at which he was scourged, with the scourges, and perched on it is the cock that crowed at Peter's denial. On the right are the hammer and nails, the basin and ewer which Pilate used to wash his hands, and the purse for the thirty pieces of silver. Hanging over the tomb is the robe in which Christ was mocked. In the background are the ghostly heads of Christ's tormentors, such as Annas and Caiaphas, Pilate and Herod, and Judas.

20b Memorial of the Holy Trinity

The Trinity is represented by two figures in human form, the Father on the left and the Son on the right, and a third, the Holy Spirit, as a dove fluttering between them. The Father raises his right hand in blessing and the Son holds a long cross in his left hand. With their other hands they both together hold a sceptre.

Around the Trinity glows a golden mandorla against a red background filled with the shapes of angels. This is the empyrean, the region of pure fire which was thought to be the abode of god and the angels. 'Empyrean' is derived from the Greek words *en*, meaning 'in', and *pyr*, meaning 'fire'. At the bottom of the miniature is the top part of a blue globe, the firmament, in which can be seen the sun, moon, and stars. God the Son's cross reaches down to touch the firmament, symbolizing the entry of God into creation by the incarnation.

38 Commemoration of St Paul

The apostle of the gentiles walks across a landscape in the foreground of which are two large rocks. In the background are water and mountains and a city. Behind St Paul hangs a red curtain. He carries the sword with which he was beheaded during the persecution of the Christians ordered by the Emperor Nero *circa* 65.

The story of Paul is well known. Although he never met Jesus Christ in the flesh, and although he has never enjoyed a great personal cult, being usually associated with St Peter, his influence on Christianity is second only to that of its founder. Christian theology is based on his epistles. He was born at Tarsus, in modern southern Turkey, a Jew of the straitest tradition. He signalized himself as a persecutor of Christians and then on the road to Damascus experienced a blinding conversion. The rest of his life was spent as a fervent evangelist for Christ. He conceived it as his special mission to bring the gospel to non-Jews and he transformed Christianity from a Jewish sect into a world religion. He made three missionary journeys, in the near east and in eastern Europe. In serious trouble at Jerusalem with his former co-religionists, the Jews, he availed himself of his rights as having been born a Roman citizen and eventually appealed to Caesar, that is, he demanded to be tried at Rome. There he was probably acquitted, for he seems to have resumed his travels before being martyred, at Rome, by beheading, since he was a Roman citizen. St Peter and St Paul have a common feast day on 29 June, and on the following day there was a subsidiary feast of Paul by himself, called his Commemoration, which was discontinued by the Roman Catholic church in 1969. On 25 January is a feast of the Conversion of St Paul.

39 Commemoration of St Leonard

The popularity of St Leonard dates from the appearance of a quite unhistorical life of him in the eleventh century. He is supposed to have lived some six hundred years before, in France. He was converted to Christianity by St Remigius, the apostle of the Franks (died 533), but refused the offer of a bishopric from Clovis, the first Christian king of the Franks. He became a monk and afterwards a hermit. By his prayers Clovis's queen was safely delivered of a child when overcome by the pangs of labour when out hunting with her husband. As a result Leonard was invoked by lying-in women.

The St Leonard in the Hastings Hours holds in his left hand a fetter. In French this is a *lien*, and there is thus a link with Leonard's name. It was asserted that whoever called upon him in prison should at once be loosed from his bonds and be able to go free and dedicate his fetters to the saint. Interest in Leonard as a deliverer of captives was increased by the fact that Bohemund, the real leader of the First Crusade and the founder of the crusading principality of Antioch, attributed his release in 1103 from imprisonment by the Moslems to the intervention of Leonard. Bohemund subsequently visited the saint's shrine near Limoges and made offerings to it. St Leonard's feast day is 6 November.

40 Memorial of St David

St David is well known as the patron of Wales and is the only Welshman to have been formally recognized as a saint, by Pope Calixtus II in 1120, but little certain is known about his life. He seems to have been an ascetic and bishop in southern Wales who died about 588. According to legend he was the son of the Prince of Cardigan, in south-west Wales. He became a priest and monk and the founder of ten monasteries in the west of Britain, including Bath, Glastonbury, and Menevia (the modern St

David's). He and his monks lived very strictly, David himself being particularly fond of total immersion in cold water as a form of asceticism. He was supposed to have travelled to Jerusalem, where he was consecrated a bishop by the patriarch, and when back in Wales to have been acclaimed archbishop of Caerleon, in southern Wales, whence he moved the seat of the diocese to Menevia. Two pilgrimages to his shrine at St David's were held to be equivalent to one pilgrimage to Rome.

St David is shown not as a bishop, but as a prince, in allusion to his royal birth. Some stories make him in fact the nephew of King Arthur: others say David was the uncle and Arthur the nephew. St David's day is 1 March.

41 Memorial of St Jerome

Jerome is seen in the character of a penitent, kneeling before a crucifix fastened to a tree and beating his breast with a stone. A Renaissance pope once commented on such a representation that it was as well for Jerome that he held his stone, which was a sign of his voluntary penance, for without this he could scarcely be considered a saint; nevertheless, Jerome is one of the great figures of Christian history.

He was born *circa* 341 and died 30 September 420. As a young man, in Rome and elsewhere, he was an ardent classical scholar. Because of an illness he renounced secular learning and became a ferocious ascetic. For five years, 374–79, he was a hermit in Syria. From 382 to 385 he was in Rome and secretary to Pope Damasus (d. 384). He then finally retired to the east, settling in Bethlehem, where he founded a monastery. To Jerome we owe the Vulgate, the most widely used version of the Bible in Latin. Jerome prepared it following on a request from Pope Damasus to revise the Latin text of the gospels. He finished it in 404.

Jerome was extreme in all things. He had a brilliant mind, he was passionate in his faith, and he had a scathing tongue. He inspired both hatred and devotion and has left behind a correspondence as historically valuable as it is lively. The red robe over a tree in the miniature alludes to the tradition that Damasus made Jerome a cardinal.

42b–43 Memorial of the Three Kings; Largesse

The number of the wise men who came from the east to worship the new-born Christ is not specified in scripture, but has become fixed by tradition at three, probably because they brought three gifts: gold, frankincense, and myrrh. From the sixth century onwards their names have become standardized in the west as Caspar, Melchior, and Balthasar, and they have been considered to have been kings. Their relics were supposed to have been discovered in Persia in the fifth century and brought to Constantinople. In the seventh century they were taken to Milan, whence, in 1162, they were removed by the Emperor Frederick Barbarossa and given to the archbishop of Cologne, who enshrined them in his cathedral. The Three Kings were venerated as patrons of travellers and pilgrims, and the first of the three prayers at their memorial in the Hastings Hours prays that the Almighty will grant 'to thy servant', at their intercession, 'on this journey, on which he is going, safety, joy, prosperity, grace, and peace, that led by thee, the true sun, the true star of the true light, he may reach his destined and desired place, safe and sound and in peace'.

Facing the miniature of the Adoration of the Magi is a page on which the beginning of the text of their memorial is bordered, or more correctly backed, by a scene of the distribution of largesse. On top of a high wall two men are throwing down coins to the populace below. One of the men is emptying the money out of a sack, the other is scattering it with his hands. The recipients are represented by a man catching coins in his hat, two men scrambling for them, a woman holding up her skirt to catch the gold, and a portly, middle-aged man holding up his hands for coins. Largesse, meaning liberality or munificence, was concretely a free bestowal of money by the king on some occasion of special rejoicing.

48b Memorial of St Christopher

A giant fords a river carrying a child on his shoulders. It is St Christopher carrying the Christ child. Christopher means 'Christ bearer' and the saint is one who despite the lack of authenticity of his story and the attacks of critics, such as Erasmus, has maintained his popularity from the middle ages down to the present day. This is because he is the particular patron of travellers; and the increase in mechanized transport, by both land and air, is thought to have increased the risks in travelling. A church in the Javel area of Paris, where Citroën cars are made, is dedicated to Christopher, and when, in 1969, the Roman Catholic church reduced his cult to a local rather than a general observance there was sharp reaction in various countries, that in Italy being led by popular film stars.

A Christopher was martyred in Asia Minor, perhaps in the third century. Everything else is legend. This tells that Christopher was a giant who resolved to serve the greatest prince in the world. He tried the most powerful king he could discover, but found that the king was afraid of the devil. So Christopher transferred his allegiance to the devil, only to discover that that personage fled in terror from the sight of a cross. When the devil had explained the significance of this, Christopher set out to find Christ. He was taught the faith by a hermit, who imposed on him the labour of carrying travellers across an especially dangerous river. One day his fare was a boy who proved to be so heavy on Christopher's shoulders that the giant could hardly make the crossing. When he had set the child down, Christopher said to him, 'If I had had the whole world on top of me, I could scarcely have felt a greater weight.' 'Do not be surprised,' came the reply, 'you have indeed borne on your shoulders not only the whole world, but also him who made it.'

St Christopher's feast day is 25 July.

50b Memorial of St Anthony

St Anthony the Great, or of Egypt (feast day, 17 January), is an important figure in the history of monasticism: a hermit who came out from total seclusion to legislate for other hermits. Popularly he was regarded as the founder of Christian monasticism. He was also renowned as a healer, because towards the end of the eleventh century there were established under his patronage the Hospitallers of St Anthony. The brethren of this order wore a dress like that of Anthony in the miniature in the Hastings Hours, that is, a dark robe marked with the Greek letter 'T', which is the tau-cross, or cross of St Anthony. They carried a little bell, as in the miniature, which they rang to attract alms. The mother house of the Hospitallers was in south-eastern France and claimed to possess the relics of the saint. These had been responsible for a miraculous cure from erysipelas. Hence had come about the foundation of the Hospitallers, hence erysipelas was known as St Anthony's fire, and hence the care of those suffering from erysipelas was the especial concern of the Hospitallers of St Anthony.

Anthony was born in Upper Egypt in 251 and died in 356. At the age of twenty he became a hermit and during his retreat from the world was a prey to extremely severe spiritual disturbances, interpreted in the idiom of the time as demoniac trials and temptations. The temptation of St Anthony is a well-known subject with artists. In the upper part of the Hastings miniature he is seen being carried aloft by a demon, while three other demons belabour him with sticks. In the background of the miniature is the meeting between St Anthony and St Paul the First Hermit, who is largely a creature of St Jerome's imagination. Paul subsisted on a piece of bread supplied daily by a raven. When Anthony visited him, the bird duly brought double rations.

53b–54 Memorial of St Erasmus; Maying

Sailors and sufferers from stomach ache share a patron saint. This is Erasmus (feast day, 2 June), about whom virtually nothing historical is known. He was probably an early bishop of Formia, in central Italy. Further, even his fictitious life says nothing of the torment usually associated with him, as in the Hastings Hours, namely having his intestines wound out on a windlass. The figure with a crown and a sceptre watching the scene could be either Diocletian or Maximinian. Erasmus is supposed to have attracted the anti-Christian attentions of both these Roman emperors at the beginning of the fourth century.

Erasmus's connexion with sailors may be due to a story that he managed to continue preaching throughout a thunderstorm, undisturbed by a thunderbolt. This endurance of weather would commend him to seamen, and the light often seen on dark tempestuous nights about the decks or rigging of ships is called St Elmo's fire after him and thought to be a sign of his protection. A windlass may then have been chosen as Erasmus's emblem because of his patronage of sailors, but later been considered to have been the instrument of his martyrdom. Because of the nature of this Erasmus was widely invoked by all with abdominal pains, including children with colic and women in labour.

In the border of the facing page is a charming scene, a boating party – it could be on the Thames at London, or on a canal at Bruges. In the boat are a man steering with an oar and drinking from a bottle and a young couple making music. Beside them are a flagon and the branch of a green tree. They have been a-maying. On May day the custom was, and still is in some places, for all, young and old, to go out into the country and return with branches of trees and flowers.

55b Memorial of St Thomas Becket

The story of Thomas Becket (b.1118) is one of the great Christian epics. The shock produced on his world by his murder on 29 December 1170 may be compared to the effect produced by the assassination of President Kennedy on 22 November 1963. Representations of Becket's death were frequent in Christian art, particularly in manuscript illumination, and the words which King Henry II is supposed to have uttered leading to the death, 'Who will rid me of this turbulent priest?', have passed into common parlance.

By birth Becket was a middle-class Londoner, who as a young man was trained and employed in the household of Theobald, archbishop of Canterbury 1138–61. When Henry II came to the throne of England in 1155, at Theobald's suggestion, he made the promising administrator chancellor of England, in effect, prime minister. The king was twenty-one, the chancellor thirty-six, and a great friendship grew up between them. Becket devoted himself wholeheartedly to the affairs of the state, not even respecting ecclesiastical preserves in the interests of secular efficiency. After Theobald died, Henry II conceived the idea that matters would be even more improved by the chancellor becoming primate. He forced Becket to become archbishop, although the other warned him that he would find him as devoted to the church as he had been to the state. This happened. Becket resigned the chancellorship, and whereas before he had lived splendidly, if never loosely, he now adopted the life of an ascetic.

The inevitable struggle with the king followed. Thomas was intransigent over the church's rights, especially her sole right to jurisdiction over the clergy, and in the end, in 1164, he appealed to the pope and went into exile. Six years later peace of a sort was patched up, and the archbishop returned to England, but his actions presaged a continuance of the earlier troubles. The king was infuriated, and four knights decided to take action. Thomas Becket was slain by them in Canterbury cathedral. Three years later he was canonized by the pope, and his shrine became the richest and most famous in Christendom.

57b Memorial of St Nicholas

This is one of the most expert miniatures in the book. Before a curtain in the apse of a church stands a bishop, mitred and carrying a crozier. It is St Nicholas, who is universally known and fêted under the name of Santa Claus.

Practically nothing is known about the historical St Nicholas, who is supposed to have been bishop of Myra, in southern Asia Minor, to have survived the persecution of Christians under the Emperor Diocletian, living into the reign of the first Christian emperor, Constantine the Great, and attending the first oecumenical council of the church, the council of Nicaea (AD 325). A church was dedicated to St Nicholas at Constantinople in the sixth century, and by the tenth century his cult had reached western Europe. He is the patron of Russia, of children and unmarried girls, of sailors, pawnbrokers, and apothecaries.

According to legend the saint once rescued three dowerless girls from prostitution by secretly giving each a bag of gold. He also restored to life three rich boys whose bodies had been concealed in a salting tub. These miracles explain Nicholas's popularity for children, and in Germanic lands it became customary to give presents to children secretly on his feast-day (6 December). This custom was transferred to Christmas and taken to America by the early Dutch settlers, where 'San Nicholaas' became 'Santa Claus'.

59b The Blessed Virgin Mary

I sing of a maiden
That is matchless:
King of all kings
To her son she chose.

He came all so still
There his mother was,
As dew in April
That falleth on the grass.

He came all so still
To his mother's bower,
As dew in April
That falleth on the flower.

He came all so still
There his mother lay,
As dew in April
That falleth on the spray.

Mother and maiden
Was never none but she:
Well may such a lady
God's mother be.

This poem dates from early fifteenth-century England. It expresses perfectly the devotion to the Virgin Mary which existed in northern Europe at the end of the Middle Ages and the beginning of the Renaissance and inspired a miniature like that of the Virgin and Child in the Hastings Hours. The maiden mother wearing a light crown is pictured gazing tenderly on her son, whom she holds in her right arm. His left hand is touching the forefinger of her left hand.

62b Memorial of St Margaret

The dying prayer of Margaret of Antioch was that all who should write or read the account of her sufferings, or celebrate her memorial, should receive pardon for any crimes they had committed; anyone who invoked her when being put to the question should be delivered; whoever dedicated a church to her, or procured lights to be burnt in her honour, should obtain anything beneficial to his salvation which he requested; and any woman who was in labour in the house of anyone who invoked the saint should have a safe birth. These petitions the Almighty is supposed to have granted, thus ensuring a wide extent to the cult of St Margaret.

In fact, the existence of Margaret appears to be wholly fictitious. Even in 494 Pope Gelasius I declared her legend apocryphal, and in 1969 the Roman Catholic church abolished her cult. The legend is that Margaret was the daughter of a pagan priest at Antioch, who turned her out of house and home when she became a Christian. She rejected the advances of the governor of Antioch and was put to torment. During her ordeal she found herself in a dark prison and prayed that her real enemy, the devil, might manifest himself so that she could strive with him openly. A dragon then appeared and tried to swallow her, but when Margaret made the sign of the cross the monster burst open and the saint escaped. She was eventually beheaded, during the persecution of the Christians which was instigated by the Emperor Diocletian in 303.

Many representations of St Margaret show her escaping through the back of the dragon. In the Hastings Hours she is at prayer in her dungeon, with the dragon menacing her at her side.

64b Memorial of St Elizabeth

In this miniature a lady in the grey dress of a Franciscan is giving alms to the poor, represented by a ragged beggar, a woman with an infant, and a pilgrim with scallop shells in his cap. Above, an angel holds two crowns, symbolizing earthly rank and heavenly rank. The grey lady is St Elizabeth of Hungary, who was born a Hungarian princess, was the wife of the ruler of Thuringia, in Germany, and died a member of the Franciscan order, at the early age of twenty-four.

Elizabeth was born in 1207, the daughter of King Andrew II of Hungary. In 1211 a marriage treaty was made between Thuringia and Hungary, by which Elizabeth was to be the bride of the heir to Thuringia. She was taken to Thuringia to be brought up and in 1221, at the age of fourteen, she married the twenty-one-year-old Landgrave Ludwig II of Thuringia. Ludwig's and Elizabeth's extremely happy married life lasted about six years. In 1227 Ludwig died, away on a crusade. Already as a girl, and even more as a wife, Elizabeth had been attracted to religion and she now gave herself entirely to acts of penance and charity. She had to leave the Thuringian court and she settled at Marburg and joined the Third Order of St Francis. She had built a hospital below the landgraves' castle of the Wartburg, and she built another at Marburg. Elizabeth died on 17 November 1231, worn out by her austerities. Pope Gregory IX canonized her in 1235.

66b–67 Memorial of St Sitha; Jousting

Sitha is a rendering of Zita, the name of a thirteenth-century Italian serving woman. She was born in 1218 at Monsagrati, a village near Lucca, in Tuscany. At the age of twelve she took service with the Fatinelli family of Lucca, with whom she remained till she died on 27 April 1272. Her piety and her habit of regarding God rather than man as her employer did not make for easy relations with her fellow servants or with her human employers. In time, though, her very real virtues won for her respect and esteem, and she achieved the position of housekeeper. After her death Zita was acclaimed a saint and invoked as the patron of housewives and domestic servants. Recourse was especially had to her for help in finding lost keys and when in danger from rivers and from crossing bridges. In the Hastings Hours she is depicted with a book in her left hand and a purse hanging from her right. The book is protected by a loose cover of material.

In the border of the facing page is a jousting scene. In a yard in a city square two men on horseback ride at each other, watched by two ladies behind the barrier of the yard. To the left, a jester sits astride the barrier. On the caparison of one of the horses are golden tears, on that of the other the French word *basir* ('kiss'). The contest has an allegorical, amatory, aspect.

68b Memorial of St Katharine

St Katharine stands, crowned, trampling on her rejected suitor the Emperor Maxentius. In her right hand is an open book and in her left the sword with which she was beheaded. To her left is the wheel – the Catherine wheel – set with razors, on which she was to have been broken, with the fire coming down from heaven which destroyed it at her prayer.

St Katharine (feast day, 25 November, suppressed by the Roman Catholic church in 1969) was the patron saint of all who make their living by disputation, such as lawyers and philosophers; of craftsmen who work with the wheel, such as millers and spinners; and of nurses, because milk instead of blood flowed from her severed head. Her story was unknown before the ninth century when her body was supposed to have been discovered at the famous monastery which was to become named after her on Mount Sinai. She was supposed to have been of royal birth and as beautiful as she was learned. The Emperor Maxentius summoned to Alexandria the fifty best advocates in the world in an attempt to dissuade her from the Christian faith, but Katharine defeated all their arguments. Maxentius tried to make her marry him, but she preferred to be the bride of Christ. She was then tortured and executed, and after her death angels came and carried her body away to Mount Sinai for burial.

70b Memorial of St Barbara

St Barbara is particularly invoked against sudden death, because of the fate of her father, who was struck dead by lightning after he had himself acted as his daughter's executioner. By extension, Barbara was thought to be especially helpful at ensuring passage from this present life fortified by the sacraments. She is also the patroness of artillerymen, fortifications, and powder magazines; architects and stonemasons; miners and prisoners.

This wide popularity is due to her story, which is quite untrustworthy. She was supposed to have been the daughter of a rich heathen who shut her up in a tower, so that no man might see her. She refused an offer of marriage brought to her by her father, and when he had a bath house built with only two windows she made the workmen add a third in honour of the Holy Trinity. Her father's inquiries about the change led to Barbara's confessing her faith. She was delated to the authorities, tortured, and beheaded by her own father.

St Barbara's day is 4 December, but it is impossible to determine whether her martyrdom should be assigned to the third century or the fourth. Her symbol is a tower, and the tower to the right of the buildings in the background of the miniature is probably meant for the tower of her imprisonment.

73b Matins: the Annunciation

The service of matins in the traditional liturgy of the western church was distinguished by the inclusion of lessons. These were usually drawn from scripture, the writings of saints, or the lives of saints. In the case of the hours of the Virgin Mary according to the use of Sarum, the lessons, which were three in number, consisted of invocations to the Virgin. This is their text, in the Hastings Hours, rendered into English from Latin.

LESSON I. Holy Virgin Mary, mother of virgins and daughter of the king of all kings, grant to us thy solace: that through thee we may be worthy to have the prize of the heavenly kingdom and to reign for ever with God's elect.

LESSON II. Holy Mary, most devout of the devout, intercede for us, thou most saintly of the saints: that through thee, O Virgin, he may receive our prayers who born of thee for us yet reigns over the heavens, so that by his love our sins may be blotted out.

LESSON III. Holy Mother of God, who wast accounted worthy to conceive him whom the whole world cannot contain, wash away our faults by thy pious intervention: that through thee we, redeemed, may be able to climb to the seat of eternal glory where thou reignest with thy son without time.

85b Lauds: the Visitation

Now the glorious mother's feast-day
  Let the faithful celebrate,
For the grace of love's devotion
  Praying all importunate,–
Love, which Mary's aged cousin
  Felt in measure passing great.

Fain to her who long was barren
  Doth the fruitful maid repair;
She, who in her secret bosom
  Doth eternal godhead bear,
Her accosts with gratulation,
  Who her saving grace doth share.

Lo, that voice, yet mute, exulteth
  As the mighty word draws nigh,
And Elizabeth confesseth
  Mary's greater dignity,
Who she passing blest declareth
  In her fruit eternally.

'What may this congratulation,'
  Meek she asks, 'forebode to me?
What this gracious salutation
  Of the king's own mother be?
And this wondrous exaltation
  Of mine unborn progeny?'

Forth a joyous strain proceedeth
From the maiden thus addrest,
Praising him who grace bestoweth
In the meek and lowly breast;
Telling how all generations
Shall from henceforth call her blest.

(English version of the Latin hymn 'Festum matris gloriosae'.)

The hymn 'Festum matris gloriosae' is probably a fifteenth-century composition and is used for the feast of the Visitation (2 July) in the Sarum Breviary printed at Venice in 1495. The miniature of the Visitation in the Hastings Hours shows St Elizabeth bending her knees so that her hand may touch the Virgin's pregnancy. In the background is Zacharias, the father of St John the Baptist.

106b Prime: the Nativity

The iconography of this scene derives from a contemporary altarpiece (*see* p. 124). As a commentary may be quoted the ancient hymn 'A solis ortus cardine', which was widely used on Christmas day in the traditional liturgy of the western church, particularly at the service of lauds. The hymn is part of a poem on the life of Christ which dates from the first half of the fifth century. It is given here in the translation from the Latin by the English hymnographer J.M. Neale (1818–68). The rest of the poem appears as a commentary on f. 119b.

From lands that see the sun arise
To earth's remotest boundaries,
The virgin-born today we sing,
The son of Mary, Christ the king.

Blest author of this earthly frame,
To take a servant's form he came,
That, liberating flesh by flesh,
Whom he had made might live afresh.

143

In that chaste parent's holy womb
Celestial grace hath found a home:
And she, as earthly bride unknown,
Yet calls that offspring blest her own.

The mansion of the modest breast
Becomes a shrine where God shall rest:
The pure and undefiled one
Conceived in her womb the Son.

Her time fufill'd, that son she bore,
Whom Gabriel's voice had told afore:
Whom, in his mother yet conceal'd,
The infant Baptist had reveal'd.

The heav'nly chorus fill'd the sky,
The angels sang to God on high,
What time to shepherds, watching lone,
They made creation's shepherd known.

113b Terce: the Annunciation to the Shepherds

Angelus inquit pastoribus,
'Nunc natus est altissimus.'

Upon a night an angel bright
Pastoribus apparuit,
And anon right, through God's might,
Lux magna illis claruit:
For love of us
(Scripture sayeth thus)
Nunc natus est altissimus.

And of that light that was so bright
Hii ualde timuerunt;
A sign of bliss to us it is,
Hec lux quam hii uiderunt:

For love of us
(Scripture sayeth thus)
Nunc natus est altissimus.

'Dread ye nothing, great joy I bring,
Quod erit omni populo,
Forwhy to you Christ is born now,
Testante euangelio.'
For love of us
(Scripture sayeth thus)
Nunc natus est altissimus.

'With good Joseph and Mary mild
Positum in presepio
Ye shall find that heavenly child
Qui celi preest solio.'
For love of us
(Scripture sayeth thus)
Nunc natus est altissimus.

The angel sang then with many more,
'Gloria in altissimis!
In earth be peace to man also
Et gaudium sit angelis.'
For love of us
(Scripture sayeth thus)
Nunc natus est altissimus.

The shepherds ran to Bethlehem then
Et inuenerunt puerum,
The which is perfect god and man
Atque saluator omnium.
For love of us
(Scripture sayeth thus)
Nunc natus est altissimus.

When in such wise found him they had
Vt dictum est per angelum,
Again they came, being full glad,

Magnificantes dominum.
For love of us
(Scripture sayeth thus)
Nunc natus est altissimus.

Now let us sing with angels
'Gloria in altissimis!'
That we may come unto that bliss
Vbi partus est uirginis,
For love of us
(Scripture sayeth thus)
Nunc natus est altissimus.

This is a macaronic poem of the later fifteenth century by the English Franciscan friar James Ryman. A macaronic poem is one in which lines in Latin are mixed with lines in the vernacular tongue of the author. The translation of the Latin above is as follows: lines 1 and 2 *The angel said to the shepherds, 'Now is born the most high'*; line 4 *Appeared to the shepherds*; line 6 *A great light shone upon them*; line 11, *They were sore afraid*; line 13 *This light which they saw*; line 18 *Which shall be to all people*; line 20 *As the gospel testifies*; line 25 *Lying in a manger*; line 27 *Who rules the throne of heaven*; lines 32 and 53 *Glory in the highest*; line 34 *And joy be among angels*; line 39 *And found the boy*; line 41 *And saviour of all*; line 46 *As was told by the angel*; line 48 *Praising the lord*; line 55 *Where is the virgin's child*. In line 19 'Forwhy' means 'because'.

119b   Sext: the Adoration of the Magi

Why, impious Herod, vainly fear
That Christ the Saviour cometh here?
He takes not earthly realms away,
Who gives the crown that lasts for aye.

To greet his birth the wise men went,
Led by the star before them sent:
Called on by light, to light they press'd,
And by their gifts their god confess'd.

In holy Jordan's purest wave
The heaven'ly lamb vouchsafed to lave:
That he, to whom was sin unknown,
Might cleanse his people from their own.

New miracle of power divine!
The water reddens into wine:
He spake the word, and pour'd the wave
In other streams than nature gave.

English version by J.M. Neale of the hymn 'Hostis Herodes impie', which is traditionally used on the feast of the Epiphany (6 January). In the western branch of Christendom the feast of the Epiphany, which originated in the east as a commemoration of the baptism of Christ, celebrates first his manifestation to the gentiles in the person of the Magi, the wise men. The theme of the baptism was taken up a week later, on the octave day of the Epiphany. Further associations of the Epiphany are with the finding of the child Jesus in the temple, directly commemorated on the first Sunday after the Epiphany, and Christ's first miracle, namely the changing of water into wine at the marriage at Cana. The miracle of Cana is directly commemorated on the second Sunday after Epiphany. The ideas of the adoration of the Magi, the baptism, and the miracle of Cana are all mentioned in the hymn above.

125b–126 None: the Presentation of Christ in the Temple; the Royal Barge

On the left-hand page is a miniature of the Virgin Mary, with St Joseph and a maidservant behind her, presenting the infant Christ to Simeon. Behind Simeon is the prophetess Anna. On the right-hand page a panel of text floats in front of a scene in which a barge is being rowed down a river near a tower. In the bow two men are standing, blowing long trumpets, which have banners bearing the royal arms of England hanging from them. These arms comprised four quarters, of which the first (top left) and the fourth (bottom right) showed the arms of France and the second (top right) and the third (bottom left) the arms of England. The positioning of the quarters is relative to the support of the flag, so that, in the miniature, where the trumpets are held horizontally, the quarters appear to the viewer opposite in order to that just given. The arms of France were, in the language of heralds, azure, three fleurs-de-lis or, that is, three golden fleurs-de-lis on a blue ground. The arms of England are gules, three lions passant guardant or, that is, three golden lions walking across a red ground, with their heads turned towards the viewer. It was Edward III of England who in 1340 adopted the arms of France in addition to those of England when he laid claim to the throne of France, towards the beginning of the Hundred Years War. The French arms remained in the royal arms of England until 1801.

In the prow of the barge is a tall flagstaff, from which flutters a long pendant in red and blue, the royal colours of England. On it is the first word 'HONI' of the famous motto of the Order of the Garter, 'HONI SOIT QUI MAL Y PENSE'. The order of the Garter, the oldest English order of chivalry, and the oldest European order, was founded on St George's day, 23 April, 1348 by King Edward III. The translation into English of its motto, which is in French, is 'Evil be to him who evil thinks.' The reasons for the adoption of the device and motto of the order are elusive. There is a well-known story that the king picked up a garter which belonged to his mistress the Countess of Salisbury, and when his knights jeered he replied that they would soon hold the garter in the highest reverence.

131b–132   Vespers: the Flight into Egypt

And when they [the wise men] were departed, behold, the angel of the Lord appeareth to Joseph in a dream, saying, Arise, and take the young child and his mother, and flee into Egypt, and be thou there until I bring thee word: for Herod will seek the young child to destroy him. When he arose he took the young child and his mother by night, and departed into Egypt. And was there until the death of Herod.

Matthew II: 13–15.

Of the four gospels only one, that of St Matthew, mentions

148

Christ's sojourn in Egypt. The Herod is Herod the Great, who was appointed king of the Jews by the Romans in 40 BC and ruled from 37 till his death in 4 BC. Christ is thought to have been born not more than three or four years before this last date. The story of the flight into Egypt attracted a number of legends, two of which are depicted in the miniature in the Hastings Hours. Half way up a hill on the right are a peasant and a field of corn. It was said that when the holy family were fleeing from Herod's soldiers they came upon a peasant sowing wheat. The Christ child reached into the bag of seed and threw some of it on to the ground. Immediately the seed grew into wheat a year old. Subsequently Herod's men arrived and asked the peasant if he had seen the fugitives. The peasant replied that he had when he was sowing the wheat. In view of the apparent age of the corn the soldiers abandoned the pursuit.

Behind the cornfield an idol falls from its pedestal. This is supposed to have been the fate of the idols which Christ passed on his way into Egypt.

139b Compline: the Massacre of the Innocents

> *All hail, ye infant martyr flowers,*
> *Cut off in life's first dawning hours,*
> *As rosebuds snapt in tempest strife*
> *When Herod sought your saviour's life.*

> *You, tender flock of Christ, we sing,*
> *First victims slain for Christ your king:*
> *Beneath the altar's heavenly ray*
> *With martyr-palms and crowns ye play.*

These two verses were translated into English by J.M. Neale from the original Latin by the Spanish poet and hymnographer Prudentius, who lived from 348 to *circa* 410. They come from a long poem of two hundred and eight lines, 'Quicumque Christum quaeritis' (All ye who seek in hope and love), on the Epiphany, which is the twelfth and last poem in Prudentius's *Cathemerinon*, a collection of hymns designed for daily use. Although the *Cathemerinon* is one of Prudentius's best works it was little used by the church in her liturgy before the sixteenth century.

150b   The Penitential Psalms: King David before the Almighty

Psalms have always been a well-spring of Christian devotion. There are one hundred and fifty of these sacred poems in the book of Psalms in the Bible, and their authorship was popularly attributed to David, the shepherd-boy who became the hero-king of Israel (d. probably *circa* 970 BC). Various psalms have distinct themes: in particular there are the seven penitential psalms, VI, XXXI, XXXVII, L, CI, CXXIX, CXLII according to the numbering in the Vulgate, but VI, XXXII, XXXVIII, LI, CII, CXXX, CXLIII according to the numbering in the original Hebrew version, which is followed by the English versions. Their incipits are VI, 'O Lord, rebuke me not in thine indignation', XXXII, 'Blessed is he whose unrighteousness is forgiven', XXXVIII, 'Put me not to rebuke, O Lord, in thine anger', LI, 'Have mercy upon me, O God, after thy great goodness', CII, 'Hear my prayer, O Lord', CXXX, 'Out of the deep have I called unto thee, O Lord', CXLIII, 'Hear my prayer, O Lord, and consider my desire'.

King David himself is especially associated with the theme of penance. This was because of his adultery with Bathsheba, the wife of Uriah the Hittite, whom he married after he had procured the death of Uriah in battle. The prophet Nathan rebuked David, who repented.

184b   Vigils of the Dead: a Funeral

At the present day death has become the great unmentionable. Earlier times were more realistic, and to keep the thought of death continually in mind was regarded as an important instrument of the spiritual life. Hence representations of funerals – one's own funeral – are found in books of hours in association with the office of the dead. English fifteenth-century feelings about death are well expressed in the following verses.

Farewell, this world! I take my leave for ever.
I am arrested to appear at God's face.
O mightiful God, thou knowest that I had liefer
Than all this world to have one hour space
To make asith for all my great trespass.
My heart, alas!, is broken for that sorrow:
Some are today that shall not be tomorrow.

This life, I see, is but a cherry fair.
All things pass, and so must I, algate.
Today I sat full royal in a chair,
Till subtle death knocked at my gate,
And, unadvised, he said to me, 'Check-mate'.
Lo! how subtle he maketh a divorce,
And worms to feed, he hath here laid my corpse.

This feeble world, so false and so unstable,
Promoteth his lovers for a little while:
But, at the last, he giveth them a bauble,
When his painted truth is turned into guile.
Experience causeth me the truth to compile,
Thinking this, too late, that I began,
For folly and hope deceiveth many a man.

Farewell, my friends, the tide abideth no man.
I must depart hence, and so shall ye.
But in this passage the best song that I can
Is 'requiem eternam'. I pray God grant it me.
When I have ended all mine adversity
Grant me in paradise to have a mansion,
That shed his blood for my redemption.
    Beati mortui qui in domino moriuntur.
    Humiliatus sum uermis.

In line 3, 'liefer' means 'rather'; in line 5, 'asith' is 'reparation'; in line 9, 'algate' means 'notwithstanding'. The two Latin words in line 25 mean 'rest eternal' and the meaning of the last two lines, which are in Latin, is, 'Blessed are the dead who die in the lord. I am humbled as a worm'.

230b Commendation of Souls: the Blessed Carried up to Heaven

Christianity is an eschatological religion, much concerned with the last things: death, judgement, heaven, and hell, as affecting both the individual soul and mankind in general. Traditionally the Christian sees his real life as being not in this world but in the next. The passage from the one world to the other therefore assumes particular importance and the church provides devotions for this, which are known as the commendation of souls. The form in which they appear in the Hastings Hours is typical. First there is the lengthy Psalm CXVIII in the Latin version, CXIX in Hebrew and English, 'Blessed are those that are undefiled in the way: and walk in the law of the Lord'. Then, after the Lord's Prayer, follow Psalm CXXXVIII (CXXXIX), 'O Lord, thou hast searched me out, and known me: thou knowest my down-sitting, and mine up-rising' (the Latin is *resurrectionem*, 'resurrection'), various suffrages, and two prayers.

The commendation of souls in the Hastings Hours is illustrated by a miniature across the bottom of which is a segment of the blue globe of the firmament, with the sun and stars. From behind appear the dead as naked figures. They are being carried aloft by angels. Above, with arms stretched out to welcome, is a half-length figure of the Almighty, wearing a tiara. There is no representation of hell in the scene, which, rather than the Last Judgment, depicts the saved being received into heaven.

250b Psalms of the Passion of the Lord: the Crucifixion

Just as certain psalms were especially associated with the theme of penance, so others were given other associations. Seven of them were considered appropriate as a devotion on the passion and crucifixion of Christ. They are Psalms XXI-XXVI, XXIX, XXX in the Latin numeration, XXII–XXVII, XXX, XXXI in the Hebrew and English. The beginning of the psalms of the passion in the Hastings Hours is faced by a miniature of the crucifixion. As a commentary on this for the present publication has been chosen a fifteenth-century poem on the cross of Christ.

Cross of Jesu Christ be ever our speed,
And keep us from peril of sins and pain.
Blessed be that Lord that on the Cross did bleed,
Christ, God, and man that for us was slain:
Dead he was, and rose up again.
Ever help us, Cross, with him to arise
From death to life, and sin to despise.

Gracious Cross, now grant us that grace
Him for to worship with all our mind
In words, in works and in every place,
Kneeling and kissing thee where we thee find.
Let us be never to him unkind,
Mercifully that made us to be men,
No more to keep but his hests ten.

O blissful Cross, teach us all virtue
Pleasing to God for our salvation,
Quenching all vices in the name of Jesu,
Ransome paying for our damnation.
Send us such grace of conversation
That we may stay and glorified be,
Where Christ is king that died on tree.

Christ that died on the holy rood,
I pray thee, good Lord, with all my might,
Send us some part of all thy good
And keep us from evil every day and night,
Continuing thy mercy, saving all right.
Title of thy passion point us safe,
As to the Cross reverence we may have.

The initial letters of the lines above make up the alphabet in the
form in which it was learned from a horn book. This was a child's
first book of letters, and derives its name from the transparent
covering of horn which was over the single page of which the book
usually consisted. The whole was fastened to a wooden frame
which had a handle. Besides the alphabet the horn book generally
gave the ten digits, some rudiments of spelling, and the Lord's

Prayer. At the beginning of a horn book stood a cross, and the first word of the poem above, which is rendered as 'Cross' there, is represented in the manuscript by a cross.

At the end of the alphabet might be an 'etc' (line 25 begins 'And', line 26 begins with a 'C'), usually three dots in a diagonal line (.·˙) which were called a tittle (the word 'Title' at the beginning of line 27 refers to this), and other punctuation marks, including a point (the word 'point' occurs in line 27). In line 21 above 'U', 'V', and 'W' are represented by the one letter 'W', the 'Ch' of 'Christ' in line 22 represents the Greek 'X', and 'I' at the beginning of line 23 is for 'Y'. 'S' at the beginning of the next line, 24, stands for 'Z'. In line 1 'speed' means 'help', 'hests' in line 14 are 'commandments', 'conversation' in line 19 means 'behaviour', and in line 20 'sty' means 'ascend'.

265b The Fifteen Prayers: Christ Washing the Disciples' Feet

The Fifteen Prayers, commonly known as the Fifteen O's because each prayer begins with 'O', are a devotion to Christ in his passion, beseeching him to have in mind the events of this. They were popularly attributed to St Bridget of Sweden (*circa* 1303–73). The opening invocations of each prayer, translated from the Latin in the Hastings Hours into English, are as follows.

O Lord Jesus Christ, eternal sweetness of those who love thee.
O Jesus, maker of the world, whom no dimension can measure with a true limit.
O Jesus, heavenly physician.
O Jesus, true liberty, paradise of the delights of angels.
O Jesus, mirror of eternal clarity.
O Jesus Christ, entirely lovable and desirable king.
O Jesus, inexhaustible fountain of piety.
O Jesus, sweetness of the heart and everlasting delight of the mind.
O Jesus, royal virtue and mental joy.
O Jesus, alpha and omega, the way, the life, the truth, and the virtue in every circumstance.

O Jesus, deepest abyss of mercy.
O Jesus, mirror of truth, sign of unity, bond of charity.
O Jesus, most strong lion, immortal and unconquered king.
O Jesus, the only begotten and high splendour of the father.
O Jesus, the true and fruitful vine.

278b–279 The Psalter of St Jerome: St Jerome; Wild Men

Daily recitation of the entire psalter of one hundred and fifty psalms was a well-known spiritual ideal, and largely as a compromise towards this end there came into being abbreviations of the psalter, of which the so-called 'Psalter of St Jerome' is one of the three main examples. It was supposed to have been compiled by St Jerome (d. 420), instructed by an angel. In fact its earliest appearance is in the tenth century.

St Jerome's life is outlined in the commentary to f.50b. He is depicted twice in the present miniature: as a small figure kneeling in penance in the background, and in the foreground seated, in the scarlet habit of a cardinal. Down the lane towards him come an ass bearing wood and a lion. The legend is that a lion was healed of a hurt paw by Jerome and his monks at Bethlehem. In gratitude the beast lived with them like a domestic animal. It was appointed to take care of the ass which fetched wood for the monastery. One day the lion fell asleep whilst the ass was grazing, and the ass was stolen. The monks suspected that the lion had yielded to its baser instincts and eaten its companion. As a punishment the lion was made to carry the wood. This it patiently tolerated, until it was able to rescue the ass and restore it to Jerome's community.

In the border opposite a wild man, with club and buckler, mounted on a monstrous bird in the water, is fighting a monster which is an armed man, with sword and shield, down to the waist. Other wild men are running down to the water's edge. The wild man was a favourite creature of mediaeval folklore. He symbolized the anti-social, irrational, repressed, antithesis to the structured, salvationist, society of the middle ages.

Description of the Manuscript

British Library, Reference Division, Department of Manuscripts, Additional MS. 54782 (formerly MS. 104 in the collection of C.W. Dyson Perrins). Book of Hours, in *Latin*, written and illuminated probably at Ghent or Bruges, before 1483, for William, Lord Hastings (beheaded 13 June 1483).

In this description the following abbreviations are used, Abb. Abbot, Abp. Archbishop, Bp. Bishop, f. folio, ff. folios, K. King, M. Martyr, Pr. Priest, V. Virgin.

G.F. Warner, *Descriptive Catalogue of Illuminated Manuscripts in the Library of C.W. Dyson Perrins*, Oxford, 1920, i, pp.236–40, ii, pl. lxxxviii. O. Pächt, 'Die niederländischen Stundenbücher des Lord Hastings', *Litterae textuales, Miniatures, Scripts, Collections, Essays Presented to G.I. Lieftinck*, IV, Leyden, 1976, pp.29–32.

Contents

(1) ff.1–12b. Calendar, written in red and black, without gradings. The noteworthy entries in red appear to be (25 August) Bernard, (28 August) Augustine, (6 October) the Translation of Hugh, (9 October) Denys, (17 November) Hugh Bp. (with an octave), (20 November) Edmund K., (1 December) Eligius, (14 December) Nichasius Bp. Entries in black include (8 January) Gudula V., (31 January) Hyacinth M., (6 February) Amand and Vedast, (20 February) Alexander Bp., (28 February) Romanus M., (2 March) Chad Bp., (4 March) Adrian Bp., (17 March) Gertrude V., (18 March) Edward, (17 April) Julian Pr., (19 April) Alphege Bp., (7 May) John Abp., (9 May) the Translation of Andrew, (19 May) Dunstan Abp., (26 May) Augustine Bp., (28 May) Germanus Bp., (5 June) Boniface Bp., (21 June) Leufred Abb., (25 June) Eligius Bp., (11 July) the Translation of Benedict, (15 July) the Translation of Swithin, (18 July) Arnulph Bp., (28 July) Pantaleon M., (31 July) Germanus Bp., (5 August) Oswald K., (31 August) Paulinus Bp., (3 September) the Ordination of Gregory, (5 September) Bertin Abb., (17 September) Lambert Bp., (25 September) Firmin Bp., (1 October) Germanus Bp., (2

October) Leodegarius Bp., (10 October) Paulinus Bp., (16 October) Michael 'in the mountain tomb', (17 October) Etheldreda, (19 October) Frideswide V., (23 October) Severinus Bp., (6 November) Leonard, (7 November) Willibrord Bp., (16 November) Edmund Bp., (3 December) Bertin Bp.

(2) ff.13–17b. Gospel extracts.

(3) ff.19–72. Devotions, consisting of a prayer to Christ, a memorial to the Trinity, Psalm LIII followed by a prayer to Christ and Psalm CXXIX, two prayers to the Virgin Mary, a prayer to Christ, the Eight Verses of St Bernard, and memorials of the following saints: Paul, Leonard, David of Wales, Jerome, the Three Kings, John the Baptist, Adrian, George, Christopher, Anthony, Fabian and Sebastian, Erasmus, Thomas Becket, Nicholas, the Virgin Mary, Anne, Margaret, Elizabeth, Sitha, Katharine, Barbara.

(4) ff.74–149b. Hours of the Virgin Mary, Sarum use ('*secundum vsum sarum*'), with appended to each hour, except to Matins, the corresponding Little Hour of the Cross. (a) ff.74–84. Matins. (b) ff.86–105b. Lauds, with memorials of the Holy Spirit, the Trinity, the Cross, Michael, John the Baptist, Peter and Paul, Andrew, John the Evangelist, Stephen, Lawrence, Thomas Becket, Nicholas, Mary Magdalen, Katharine, Margaret,

the Relics of the Saints, All Saints, and Peace. (c) ff.107–112b. Prime. (d) ff.114–118b. Terce. (e) ff.120–124. Sext. (f) ff.126–130. None. (g) ff.132–138b. Vespers. (h) ff.140–149b. Compline, followed by devotions to the Virgin Mary.

(5) ff.151–183b. Penitential Psalms, Gradual Psalms, and Litany. The litany invokes twenty martyrs, none of whom appear to have local or personal significance; twenty-four confessors, including (x) Livinus, (xi) Leonard, (xii) Bernard, (xiii) Francis, (xiv) Louis, (xv) Bernardine, (xvi) Edward, (xvii) Isidore, (xviii) Julian, (xix) Gildard, (xx) Medard, (xxiii) Swithin, (xxiv) Birinus; and twenty-seven virgins, including (viii) Clare, (xii) Elizabeth, (xxi) Wilgefortis, (xxii) Itisberga, (xxiv) Sitha.

(6) ff.185–229b. Office of the Dead, Sarum use.

(7) ff.231–249. Commendation of Souls.

(8) ff.251–264b. Psalms of the Passion.

(9) ff.266–275b. The Fifteen Prayers.

(10) ff.276–297b. The Psalter of St Jerome.

Vellum and paper; ff.iii + 300 (last three blank) 16·5 × 12·3 cm.

Writing
The basic scheme of the gatherings is two ternions for the calendar and quaternions elsewhere, with one gathering of four leaves (ff.260–264), one of ten

157

(ff.291–300), and five additions of
single folios (ff.37, 149, 183, 249,
251) for the sake of textual
divisions and completeness.
Further, thirty-five full-page and
four half-page miniatures on
single folios were inserted. The
four half-page miniatures form a
gathering of their own (ff.38–41).
Seven full-page miniatures have
been lost, so that twenty-eight
remain (ff.18b, 20b, 42b, 48b, 50b,
53b, 55b, 57b, 59b, 62b, 64b, 66b,
68b, 70b, 73b, 85b, 106b, 113b,
119b, 125b, 131b, 139b, 150b,
184b, 230b, 250b, 265b, 278b).
The present collation of the
manuscript is therefore i⁶, ii⁶, iii¹⁰
(6 and 8 insertions), iv⁸, v⁷ (7 an
insertion), vi⁴, vii¹¹ (1, 7, and 9
insertions), viii¹⁵ (1, 3, 5, 7, 10, 12,
14 insertions), ix¹¹ (1, 3, 6
insertions), x⁸ (6 and 7 insertions),
xi⁸, xii⁸, xiii⁹ (4 an insertion), xiv¹⁰
(2 and 8 insertions), xv⁹(4 an
insertion), xvi¹⁰ (1 and 9
insertions), xvii⁹ (9 an insertion),
xviii⁹ (1 an insertion), xix⁸, xx⁸,
xxi⁹ (9 an insertion), xxii⁹ (1 an
insertion), xxiii–xxvi⁸, xxvii⁸ (3
and 6 insertions), xxviii⁸, xxix⁸,
xxx¹¹ (1, 2, 3 insertions), xxxi⁴,
xxxii⁹ (1 an insertion), xxxiii⁹ (5 an
insertion), xxxiv⁸, xxxv¹⁰. Ruled
for sixteen lines to a page, except in
calendar where there are seventeen.
Written in *lettre bourguignonne*.
Second folio (after calendar)
'-*monium ut testimonium*'. Simple
decorated initials at beginning of
lesser items in text, more elaborate
ones at major divisions. Some
simple line endings.

Miniatures and Borders
There are twenty-eight full-page
miniatures each surrounded by an
ornamental border and faced by a
text-page surrounded by an
ornamental, or in five cases (ff.43,
54, 67, 126, 279) historiated,
border and four half-page
miniatures (ff.38, 39, 40, 41), each
having also six lines of text on the
page and surrounded by an
ornamental border. Further, there
are seven text-pages with
ornamental borders (ff.13, 26, 45,
46, 47, 52, 61) which survive
without facing miniatures, which
have been lost. The subjects of the
miniatures, and historiated
borders, are as follows.

1. f.18b. The mass of St
Gregory. 2. f.20b. The Trinity.
3. f.38. St Paul. 4. f.39. St
Leonard. 5. f.40. St David of
Wales. 6. f.41. St Jerome. 7. f.42b.
The Adoration of the Magi. f.43.
Historiated border: Largesse.
8. f.48b. St Christopher. 9. f.50b.
St Anthony. 10. f.53b. St
Erasmus. f.54. Historiated border:
Maying. 11. f.55b. St Thomas
Becket. 12. f.57b. St Nicholas.
13. f.59b. The Virgin and Child.
14. f.62b. St Margaret. 15. f.64b.
St Elizabeth of Hungary.
16. f.66b. St Sitha. f.67.
Historiated border: Jousting.
17. f.68b. St Katharine. 18. f.70b.
St Barbara. 19. f.73b. The
Annunciation. 20. f.85b. The
Visitation. 21. f.106b. The
Nativity. 22. f.113b. The
Annunciation to the Shepherds.
23. f.119b. The Adoration of the

Magi. 24. f.125b. The Presentation of Christ in the Temple. f.126. Historiated border: The Royal Barge. 25. f.131b. The Flight into Egypt. 26. f.139b. The Massacre of the Innocents. 27. f.150b. King David before the Almighty. 28. f.184b. A Funeral. 29. f.230b. The Blessed Carried up to Heaven. 30. f.250b. The Crucifixion. 31. f.265b. Christ Washing the Disciples' Feet. 32. f.278b. St Jerome. f.279. Historiated border: Wild Men.

Binding

Modern, red morocco richly tooled, with lining of white watered silk decorated with light sprig-work in red. Gilt gauffered edges.

History

Purchased by C.W. Dyson Perrins from the booksellers Bernard Quaritch, 3 January 1910, for £2200. Dyson Perrins' bookplate and the number in his collection, 104, are on a fly-leaf at the beginning of the manuscript (f.i). On a fly-leaf at the end (f.iii) is an earlier numbering in Dyson Perrins' collection, viz., 26. Retained by Mrs C.W. Dyson Perrins when her husband's collection of illuminated manuscripts was dispersed after his death (29 January 1958) and bequeathed to the British Museum on her death (28 December 1968).